# UNITED STATES HISTORY

*for Christian Schools*®

Terri L. Koontz
Lynn Garland


Bob Jones University Press
Greenville, South Carolina 29614

**Photograph Credits**
The following agencies and individuals have furnished materials to meet the photographic needs of this textbook. We wish to express our gratitude to them for their important contribution.

DigitalSTOCK
International Herald Tribune, The
Library of Congress

Oxford University Press
PhotoDisc, Inc.
Unusual Films

**Cover**
Unusual Films (Front left, spine, back)
DigitalSTOCK (Front right)

PhotoDisc, Inc. 21; Unusual Films 35; Library of Congress LC-USZ62-056944 53 (left), LC-USZ62-121242 53 (right); Oxford University Press 76; International Herald Tribune, The 103

NOTE:
The fact that materials produced by other publishers are referred to in this volume does not constitute an endorsement by Bob Jones University Press of the content or theological position of materials produced by such publishers. The position of Bob Jones University Press, and the University itself, is well known. Any references and ancillary materials are listed as an aid to the student or the teacher and in an attempt to maintain the accepted academic standards of the publishing industry.

**Student Activities in UNITED STATES HISTORY for Christian Schools®**

**For use with UNITED STATES HISTORY for Christian Schools,® Third Edition**

**Terri Koontz**
**Lynn Garland**

| **Compositor** | **Cover and Design** | **Illustrators** | **Project Editor** |
| Kelley Moore | Joseph Tyrpak | Jim Hargis | Manda Kalagayan |
| | | Kathy Pflug | |

Produced in cooperation with the Bob Jones University Department of History of the College of Arts and Science, the School of Religion, and Bob Jones Academy.

*for Christian Schools* is a registered trademark of Bob Jones University Press.

© 1993, 2001 Bob Jones University Press
Greenville, South Carolina 29614
First Edition © 1993 Bob Jones University Press



ISBN 1-57924-643-5

15  14  13  12  11  10  9  8  7  6  5  4  3  2  1

# CONTENTS

# Unit VII: Challenge

# UNITED STATES HISTORY

Name ____________________

Chapter 1    Activity 1

## Think About It!

**Use a dictionary or an encyclopedia to help you answer these questions.**

The Indians had a custom called "potlatch" in which they would give a dinner and gifts to visitors. They did this expecting gifts in return. How do you think confusion about this custom could have caused tension between the Indians and the explorers?

________________________________________

________________________________________

________________________________________

________________________________________

________________________________________

For almost two hundred years the Europeans went on Crusades to rid the Holy Land of "infidels." How did this practice eventually lead to the discovery and exploration of the New World, and how did it affect the treatment of the people they found there?

________________________________________

________________________________________

________________________________________

________________________________________

________________________________________

The Micmac Indians of Canada normally used what they needed from the land and left the rest. After the arrival of the French, however, the Indians began to deplete the beaver population to near extinction in their area. What caused them to change their normal way of hunting?

________________________________________

________________________________________

________________________________________

________________________________________

________________________________________

# UNITED STATES HISTORY



Chapter 1     Activity 2

## Map Study: Explorations of the New World

**Refer to the map on page 5 and the text.**

**In the blank to the left of the explorer's name, write the letter from the map below that corresponds to the route that explorer took on his travels. In the blank to the right of his name, write the name of the country for which he explored and the year he began his exploration.**

_______ 1. Cabot                    _________________________________

_______ 2. Columbus              _________________________________

_______ 3. Coronado             _________________________________

_______ 4. Cortés                  _________________________________

_______ 5. De Soto               _________________________________

_______ 6. Drake                    _________________________________

_______ 7. Magellan              _________________________________

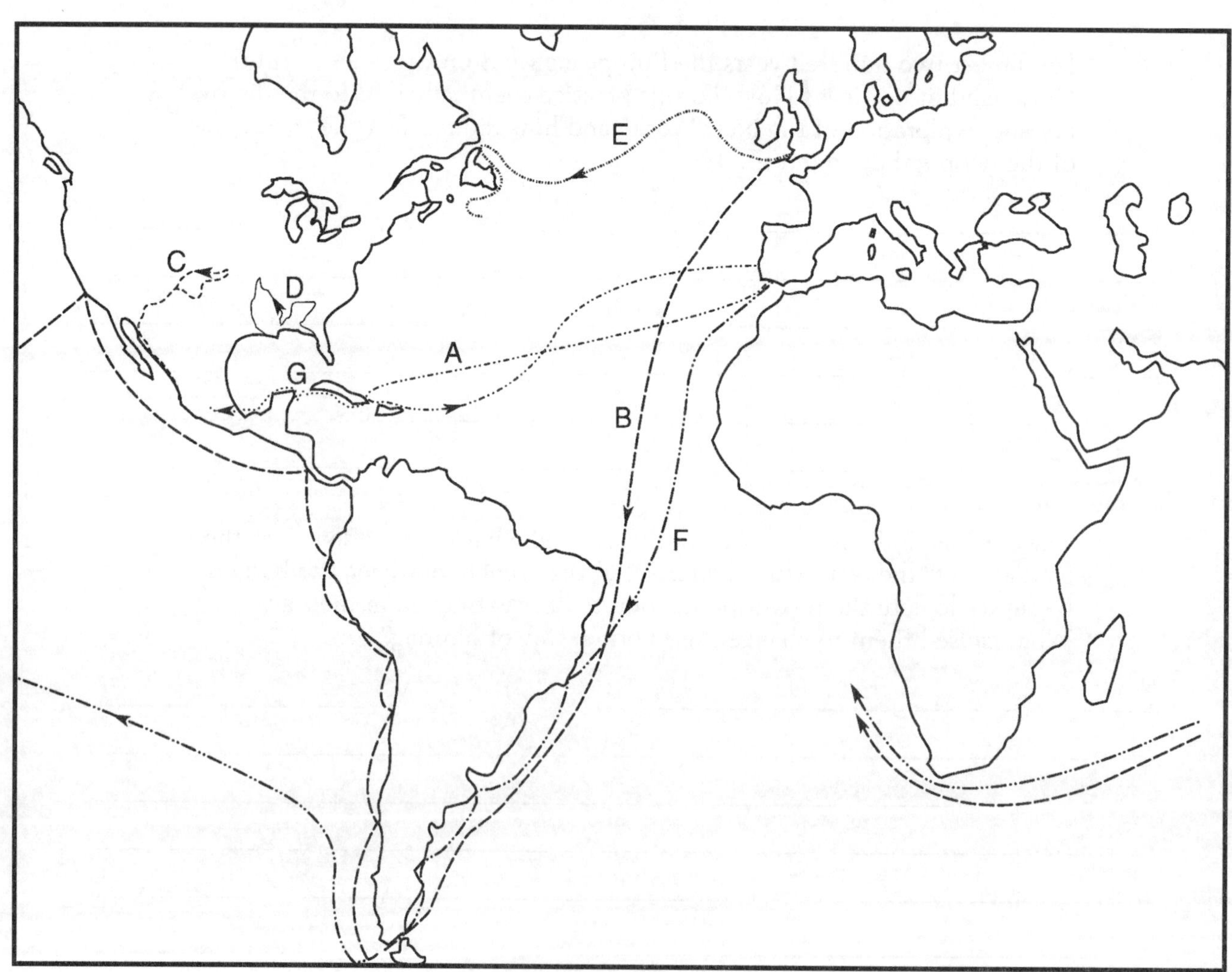

## Read and Heed

The early Virginia settlers came to America with dreams of prosperity and wealth. They had heard of the Spanish conquest of South America's gold and silver and of the Indian laborers to be had. When they arrived in America, they found life much more difficult than they expected. Rather than working hard to become self-sufficient, the colonists chose to work about four hours a day and relax and entertain themselves the rest of the time. After a winter in which sixty out of one hundred colonists died, Captain John Smith took charge and enforced with punishment the biblical rule "if any would not work, neither should he eat" (II Thess. 3:10).

**Find eight other verses that warn about laziness. Write the reference and the principle for living found there.**

|  | *REFERENCE* | *LIFE PRINCIPLE* |
|---|---|---|
| 1. | | |
| 2. | | |
| 3. | | |
| 4. | | |
| 5. | | |
| 6. | | |
| 7. | | |
| 8. | | |

## Who Am I?

**Read each statement and decide who would have said it. Write the correct answer in the blank.**

_______________________  1. I wrote a travel-log of a famous explorer with whom I shared a prison cell.

_______________________  2. I set sail from Spain with three hundred men and five ships. Three years later, one of my ships arrived home with only eighteen original crew members left.

_______________________  3. I disobeyed the governor of Cuba and conquered the richest Indian tribe in Mexico.

_______________________  4. I told of my adventures in China and of a land called Cipangu, which was reportedly paved with gold.

_______________________  5. I, Giovanni, reached Newfoundland in search of China. To the English, I was known by a different name.

_______________________  6. My calculations were faulty, but I thought I could sail three thousand miles west to reach China.

_______________________  7. Romans 1:17 ("The just shall live by faith") transformed my life and teachings.

_______________________  8. In my ship, *The Golden Hind*, I fought the Catholic threat on the high seas with my cousin Sir John Hawkins.

_______________________  9. Second Thessalonians 3:10 ("If any would not work, neither should he eat") was a verse I enforced to ensure Jamestown's survival.

_______________________ 10. In a Spanish attempt to settle the southeastern United States, I was the first to explore the Florida peninsula in 1513.

_______________________ 11. A German mapmaker named the New World after me instead of after Columbus.

_______________________ 12. I searched for the Seven Cities of Cibola and found the Grand Canyon.

_______________________ 13. A cargo of spices worth sixty times the cost of my expedition was my reward for sailing to India.

_______________________ 14. I financed two attempts to colonize the New World in an area that I called Virginia.

_______________________ 15. I landed at Tampa Bay, traveled to North Carolina, and eventually discovered the Mississippi River.

_______________________ 16. I helped bring peace to Jamestown by marrying an Indian chief's daughter.

_______________________ 17. I went to England for supplies, and when I returned, I found the town of Raleigh empty.

_______________________ 18. I was the first to round the southern cape of Africa.

*Not assigned Review*

## The New World

**Read each question carefully. Write the answers in the blanks and then unscramble the numbered letters to find the mystery word.**

1. Promoters tried to attract settlers to Virginia by calling it

   __ __ __ __ __  __ __ __ __ __ __ __ __ __.
                1

2. A movement that rediscovered biblical truth and shattered the religious monopoly of Rome was known as the

   __ __ __ __ __ __ __ __ __ __ __.
          2

3. Unfortunately, this king lured the Spanish to conquer his kingdom by offering rich farewell gifts.

   __ __ __ __ __ __ __ __ __.
         3

4. What was the nickname Queen Elizabeth I gave to John Hawkins and Francis Drake?

   __ __ __ __ __ __ __.
       4

5. Who was the explorer for whom the New World was named?

   __ __ __ __ __ __ __ __ __ __ __ __ __ __ __.
          5

6. What is the name of the company that made only one attempt to colonize Maine?

   __ __ __ __ __ __ __ __  __ __ __ __ __ __ __.
         6

7. The large force of Spanish ships that attempted to conquer England was called the

   __ __ __ __ __ __ __ __  __ __ __ __ __ __ __.
           7

8. What was the name Columbus gave the island on which he landed?

   __ __ __  __ __ __ __ __.
      8

9. The Indian nation which was conquered by Cortés was the

   __ __ __ __ __ __.
      9

### *MYSTERY WORD*

The New World promised wealth, freedom, and

__ __ __ __ __ __ __ __ __.

## What Comes Next?

**Place the following events in their correct order using the spaces provided below.**

A. Jamestown—first permanent English settlement
B. Beginning of Protestant Reformation with Martin Luther
C. Dias sails along African coast and names the southern cape Good Hope
D. Ponce de León explores the Florida peninsula
E. Virginia House of Burgesses is established
F. Cabot's sail to Newfoundland establishes English North American claims
G. Hernando Cortés conquers Aztec city of Tenochtitlán
H. Roanoke Island (Lost Colony)
 I. Rustichello writes of Marco Polo's experiences
 J. Vasco da Gama sails to India and returns with expensive spice cargo
K. Spanish Armada is launched against England
L. Christopher Columbus discovers New World
M. Sir Francis Drake begins world voyage
N. Magellan begins his voyage around the Earth

1. ___________________________________________
2. ___________________________________________
3. ___________________________________________
4. ___________________________________________
5. ___________________________________________
6. ___________________________________________
7. ___________________________________________
8. ___________________________________________
9. ___________________________________________
10. ___________________________________________
11. ___________________________________________
12. ___________________________________________
13. ___________________________________________
14. ___________________________________________

## Providence Praised

**Read this excerpt from William Bradford's *Of Plymouth Plantation* and then answer the questions on the next page.**

Having found a good haven and being brought safely in sight of land, they fell upon their knees and blessed the God of Heaven who had brought them over the vast and furious ocean, and delivered them from all the peril and miseries of it, again to set their feet upon the firm and stable earth, their proper element.

But here I cannot but make a pause, and stand half amazed at this poor people's present condition; and so I think will the reader, too, when he considers it well. Having thus passed the vast ocean, and that sea of troubles before while they were making their preparations, they now had no friends to welcome them, nor inns to entertain and refresh their weather-beaten bodies, nor houses—much less towns—to repair to.

It is recorded in Scripture (Acts, xxviii) as a mercy to the Apostle and his shipwrecked crew, that the barbarians showed them no small kindness in refreshing them; but these savage barbarians when they met with them were readier to fill their sides full of arrows than otherwise! As for the season, it was winter, and those who have experienced the winters of the country know them to be sharp and severe, and subject to fierce storms when it is dangerous to travel to known places—much more to search an unknown coast. Besides, what could they see but a desolate wilderness, full of wild beasts and wild men; and what multitude there might be of them they knew not! Neither could they, as it were, go up to the top of Pisgah, to view from this wilderness a more goodly country to feed their hopes; for which way soever they turned their eyes (save upward to the heavens!) they could gain little solace from any outward objects. Summer being done, all things turned upon them a weatherbeaten face; and the whole country, full of woods and thickets, presented a wild and savage view.

If they looked behind them, there was the mighty ocean which they had passed, and was now a gulf separating them from all civilized parts of the world. If it be said that they had their ship to turn to, it is true; but what did they hear daily from the captain and crew. That they should quickly look out for a place with their shallop, where they would be not far off; for the season was such that the captain would not approach nearer to the shore till a harbor had been discovered which he could enter safely; and that the food was being consumed apace, but he must and would keep sufficient for the return voyage. It was even muttered by some of the crew that if they did not find a place in time, they would turn them and their goods ashore and leave them.

Let it be remembered, too, what small hope of further assistance from England they had left behind them, to support their courage in this sad condition and the trials they were under; for how the case stood between the settlers and the merchants at their departure has already been described. It is true, indeed, that the affection and love of their brethren at Leyden towards them was cordial and unbroken; but they had little power to help them or themselves.

What, then, could now sustain them but the spirit of God, and His grace? Ought not the children of their fathers rightly to say: Our fathers were Englishmen who came over the great ocean, and were ready to perish in this wilderness; but they cried unto the Lord, and He heard their voice, and looked on their adversity. . . . Let them therefore praise the Lord, because He is good, and His mercies endure forever. Yea, let them that have been redeemed of the Lord, show how He hath delivered them from the hand of the oppressor. When they wandered forth into the desert wilderness, out of the way, and found no city to dwell in, both hungry and thirsty, their soul was overwhelmed in them. Let them confess before the Lord His loving kindness, and His wonderful works before the sons of men!

1. Look up and define the following words.

   shallop ______________________________________________________________

   apace ________________________________________________________________

2. Look up Deuteronomy 34:1. How does the reference to Mt. Pisgah fit with the
   allusion in paragraph three? ______________________________________________

   ____________________________________________________________________

   ____________________________________________________________________

3. After reading paragraph four, how would you describe the captain's and crew's
   feelings toward the Pilgrims? ____________________________________________

   ____________________________________________________________________

   ____________________________________________________________________

4. What feelings (implied in paragraph five) were between the settlers and merchants
   when the Pilgrims left England? __________________________________________

   ____________________________________________________________________

   ____________________________________________________________________

5. For extra credit, identify the psalm that Bradford paraphrases in the final paragraph.

   ____________________________________________________________________

6. Write a first-person narrative paragraph about your first impressions and hopes for the
   new land. Write from the perspective of Joseph or Priscilla Mullins, two children who
   came over on the *Mayflower* with their parents.

   ____________________________________________________________________

   ____________________________________________________________________

   ____________________________________________________________________

   ____________________________________________________________________

   ____________________________________________________________________

   ____________________________________________________________________

   ____________________________________________________________________

   ____________________________________________________________________

   ____________________________________________________________________

   ____________________________________________________________________

   ____________________________________________________________________

   ____________________________________________________________________

   ____________________________________________________________________

   ____________________________________________________________________

## Mayflower Compact Impact

**Read the Mayflower Compact below and compare it with the Preamble of the U.S. Constitution, which can be found on page 662 of the textbook.**

In the name of God, Amen. We, whose names are underwritten, the loyal subjects of our dread sovereigne Lord, King James, by the grace of God, of Great Britaine, France, and Ireland king, defender of the faith, etc., having undertaken, for the glory of God, and advancement of the Christian faith, and honour of our king and country, a voyage to plant the first colony in the Northerne parts of Virginia, doe, by these presents solemnly and mutually in the presence of God, and one of another, covenant and combine ourselves together into a civill body politick, for our better ordering and preservation and furtherance of the ends aforesaid; and by virtue hereof to enacte, constitute, and frame such just and equall laws, ordinances, acts, constitutions, and offices, from time to time, as shall be thought most meete and convenient for the generall good of the Colonie unto which we promise all due submission and obedience. In witness whereof we have hereunder subscribed our names at Cap-Codd the 11 of November, in the year of the raigne of our sovereigne lord, King James, of England, France, and Ireland, the eighteenth, and of Scotland the fifte-fourth. Anno. Dom. 1620.

1. What is the significance of the Mayflower Compact to the United States government as a whole? _______________________________________________

   _______________________________________________

   _______________________________________________

2. Compare the similarities of the Mayflower Compact and the Constitution Preamble.

| *Mayflower Compact* | *Constitution Preamble* |
| --- | --- |
| a) ____________________ | ____________________ |
| ____________________ | ____________________ |
| b) ____________________ | ____________________ |
| ____________________ | ____________________ |
| c) ____________________ | ____________________ |
| ____________________ | ____________________ |
| d) ____________________ | ____________________ |
| ____________________ | ____________________ |

## Map Study: Settlement of the Colonies

**Refer to the maps on pages 21, 28, and 30 as well as an atlas and the text to complete the map below.**

1. Label each of the original thirteen colonies with the complete name of the colony.
2. Identify the New England Colonies, including the disputed territory; the Middle Colonies; and the Southern Colonies. Color each section a different color and make a key to fit your colors.
3. Label the following settlements by placing a small dot on the map and then writing the name of the settlement beside the dot.
   - Baltimore
   - Boston
   - Charleston
   - Jamestown
   - New York City
   - Philadelphia
4. Below the colony names, write the name(s) of the founder(s).

A. New Hampshire

___________________

___________________

B. Massachusetts

___________________

___________________

C. Connecticut

___________________

D. Rhode Island

___________________

___________________

E. New York

___________________

___________________

___________________

F. Pennsylvania

___________________

G. Maryland

___________________

___________________

H. The Carolinas

___________________

I. Georgia

___________________

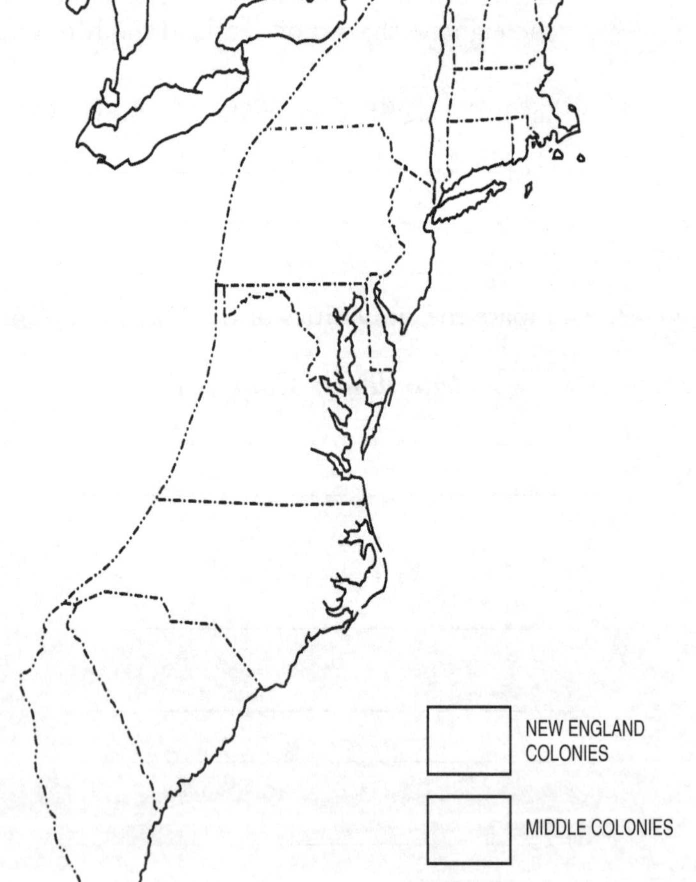

Name _______________________

## Choices, Choices

**Choose one of the original colonies. Research its history and complete the following activity based upon the information obtained.**

1. Colony name _______________________________________________

2. Climate type _______________________________________________

3. Main income source in the colony _______________________________

4. Common foods that would have been grown and eaten _______________
_______________________________________________________________

5. Occupation best suited to the colony ____________________________

6. List five items that you would have wanted to bring with you to the colony and tell why they would have been important. ____________________________
_______________________________________________________________
_______________________________________________________________
_______________________________________________________________
_______________________________________________________________
_______________________________________________________________

7. Write a letter to your parents in England telling them why your choice to come to this colony was a good one and telling them what problems you have encountered.
_______________________________________________________________
_______________________________________________________________
_______________________________________________________________
_______________________________________________________________
_______________________________________________________________
_______________________________________________________________
_______________________________________________________________
_______________________________________________________________
_______________________________________________________________
_______________________________________________________________
_______________________________________________________________
_______________________________________________________________
_______________________________________________________________
_______________________________________________________________
_______________________________________________________________

## Colonial Order

**Put the correct letter in the blank provided.**

________ 1. A colony that was governed by a trade company was a
    A. royal colony.
    B. proprietary colony.
    C. trade colony.
    D. charter colony.

________ 2. An indenture was
    A. a work contract.
    B. a fifty-acre land tract.
    C. a set of wooden false teeth.
    D. a servant.

________ 3. The belief that outward obedience to the Scripture was unnecessary to show an inner relationship to Christ was called
    A. Fundamental Orders.
    B. Concessions and Agreements.
    C. Antinomianism.
    D. Predestination.

________ 4. "Precious stink" was a description of America's first cash crop.
    A. tobacco
    B. cauliflower
    C. cabbage
    D. corn

________ 5. "Holy Experiment" refers to the state of
    A. Delaware.
    B. Pennsylvania.
    C. Maryland.
    D. New York.

________ 6. If someone paid for his passage to the New World, the Virginia Company offered him
    A. a patroon.
    B. an indenture.
    C. a work contract.
    D. headrights.

________ 7. The group of settlers who came from Scrooby, England, then moved to Holland, and finally settled in Massachusetts was called the
    A. Anglicans.
    B. Separatists.
    C. Puritans.
    D. fundamentalists.

________ 8. The man who dreamed of a "wilderness Zion" in Massachusetts was
    A. William Bradford.
    B. Thomas Hooker.
    C. Roger Williams.
    D. John Winthrop.

________ 9. This document has been called the first written constitution in America.
    A. Fundamental Orders of Connecticut
    B. Law, Concessions, and Agreements
    C. Mayflower Compact
    D. Toleration Act of 1649

________ 10. The man who discovered a waterway from below Long Island to Albany, New York, was
    A. Henry Hudson.
    B. Peter Stuyvesant.
    C. Peter Minuit.
    D. Cecilius Calvert.

________ 11. Thomas Hooker moved three congregations into the Connecticut River valley to form what was collectively called the
    A. Massachusetts Bay Company.
    B. Puritan Plurality.
    C. River Colony.
    D. Mystic River Towns.

________ 12. The contract of government drawn up by those on the *Mayflower* was known as the
    A. Plymouth Plan.
    B. Mayflower Compact.
    C. Articles of Agreement.
    D. Separatist Doctrine.

## Eastern Indian Tribes

**Choose one of the following Eastern Indian tribes. Using outside resources, answer the following questions about the chosen tribe.**

| | | | | |
|---|---|---|---|---|
| Cherokee | Alabama | Algonquin | Delaware | Erie |
| Fox | Chickasaw | Creek | Iowa | Menominee |
| Miami | Huron | Illinois | Ojibwa | Osage |
| Missouri | Sauk | Mohican | Powhatan | Potawatomi |
| Ottawa | Yamasee | Natchez | Catawba | Susquehanna |
| Quapaw | Shawnee | | | |

1. Where in the Eastern United States was the tribe located? _______________
   _____________________________________________________________

2. What are some interesting facts about the tribe's culture? _______________
   _____________________________________________________________
   _____________________________________________________________
   _____________________________________________________________

3. What type of government did the tribe have? _______________
   _____________________________________________________________
   _____________________________________________________________

4. What is the earliest known contact between the tribe and Europeans? _______
   _____________________________________________________________
   _____________________________________________________________

5. Were there any well-known members of the tribe? If so, who were they, and why
   were they well known? _______________________________________________
   _____________________________________________________________
   _____________________________________________________________

6. Were there any unique facts about the tribe not previously known? _________
   _____________________________________________________________
   _____________________________________________________________
   _____________________________________________________________

7. Are members of this tribe living today, and if so where? _______________
   _____________________________________________________________
   _____________________________________________________________
   _____________________________________________________________

## Native Americans

**Put the correct answers in the blanks provided.**

1. What two major groups of Mound Builders lived in North America? ______________
   ______________________________________________

2. List one effigy mound and one fortification mound. ______________________
   ______________________________________________

3. What were the six tribes who joined together to form the Iroquois Confederacy?
   ______________________________________________
   ______________________________________________

4. Who persuaded the tribes to come together in peace? ______________________
   ______________________________________________
   ______________________________________________

5. What were the chiefs called? ______________________

6. Who ruled over the longhouse? ______________________
   ______________________________________________

7. What native crop discovered by Columbus has become one of the four most important foods in the world? ______________________

8. How did the Indians clear the land of trees? ______________________
   ______________________________________________
   ______________________________________________

9. What did some tribes use as a scarecrow? ______________________
   ______________________________________________
   ______________________________________________

10. How did the Indians' corn differ from today's corn and why? ______________________
    ______________________________________________
    ______________________________________________

## Who and What

**Use complete sentences to answer the following who or what questions.**

1. What group of people did Benjamin Franklin refer to as "aliens"?

   _______________________________________________________________

2. What Iroquois Indian trail did the early settlers use to migrate to the South?

   _______________________________________________________________

3. What were two epidemics that seriously reduced the New England population?

   _______________________________________________________________

4. Who was the Puritan pastor who promoted inoculation to prevent disease?

   _______________________________________________________________

5. What toy reflected the high mortality rate among colonial children?

   _______________________________________________________________

   _______________________________________________________________

6. From what is colonial architectural style copied?

   _______________________________________________________________

7. What was the paddle-shaped board used as a child's first book?

   _______________________________________________________________

8. From what did it (#7) get its name?

   _______________________________________________________________

   _______________________________________________________________

9. From what text is "In Adam's fall, we sinned all" taken?

   _______________________________________________________________

10. What was a school taught by a widow or a spinster?

    _______________________________________________________________

11. What was the 1769 New York advertisement talking about when it said it "saved many from drowning"?

    _______________________________________________________________

12. What staple food, first discovered in Peru, went to Europe and came back to North America in the 1700s?

    _______________________________________________________________

13. What was the purpose of education in the 1700s?

    _______________________________________________________________

    _______________________________________________________________

## The Servant and the Slave

**Use the text and an encyclopedia to help you compare and contrast the life of an indentured servant and that of a slave.**

<table>
<tr><td>SERVANT</td><td></td><td>SLAVE</td></tr>
<tr><td></td><td>Family Life</td><td></td></tr>
<tr><td></td><td>Treatment</td><td></td></tr>
<tr><td></td><td>Social Life</td><td></td></tr>
<tr><td></td><td>Work</td><td></td></tr>
<tr><td></td><td>Future Prospects</td><td></td></tr>
</table>

## False Alarms

**Circle the appropriate letter to identify the statement as true or false. If the statement is false, correct it.**

T    F    1. Malaria claimed lives in South Carolina in the early colonial days.

_______________________________________________________________

T    F    2. A subsistence crop is a crop produced to raise money.

_______________________________________________________________

T    F    3. A pennysheet was paper money equivalent to a penny.

_______________________________________________________________

T    F    4. Passage to the New World was sometimes paid for by indenture.

_______________________________________________________________

T    F    5. Linsey-woolsey was the fuzz that collected when the women wove cloth.

_______________________________________________________________

T    F    6. If your fire went out, you could borrow a "chunk of fire."

_______________________________________________________________

T    F    7. Wigs were popular only with bald men.

_______________________________________________________________

T    F    8. The "bagwig" was carried in a linen bag for emergency use.

_______________________________________________________________

T    F    9. A wig was "dressed" with ribbons and curls.

_______________________________________________________________

T    F   10. Philadelphia established the first public library in America in 1698.

_______________________________________________________________

T    F   11. A favorite American beverage after the Boston Tea Party was hot cocoa.

_______________________________________________________________

T    F   12. Puritans wore bright clothing and enjoyed good music.

_______________________________________________________________

T    F   13. Women in the colonies married much later than women in Europe.

_______________________________________________________________

T    F   14. A popular addition to colonial plantations was a roofed porch called a piazza.

_______________________________________________________________

T    F   15. The late seventeenth-century infant death rate in the colonies was significantly
          lower than in Europe.

_______________________________________________________________

## Crossword Puzzle

**Complete the following crossword puzzle.**

### ACROSS

3. standard fare on frontier farm dinner tables
5. a three-legged, covered pot
6. toppings for well-dressed colonial men
9. a single page of a book sold for a penny
10. end of the Great Philadelphia Wagon Road
11. one common social event on the frontier
13. bondsman
16. one of the large groups of non-English settlers
18. a group from Germany, not the Netherlands
19. common name for village school
21. mixture of linen and wool
24. *Poor Richard's* author
25. South Carolina grain crop
26. urged smallpox inoculations

### DOWN

1. cornbread made from meal and sour milk
2. Indian crop made popular worldwide
4. common home in the colonial backcountry
6. reigns at thirty years of age (*Poor Richard's*)
7. roofed porch on a southern home
8. Education should provide the ability to read this.
12. Poor Richard says, "Plow deep while sluggards __."
14. catches few flies (*Poor Richard's*)
15. A budget wig was called the __ *Buckle.*
17. "Williamsburg style" or "__ style"
20. paddle-shaped "book" made of this
22. time to go to bed and to rise (*Poor Richard's*)
23. "makes waste" (*Poor Richard's*)

## Map Study: Religion in the Colonies

**Refer to the map on pages x and xi as well as to the text to complete the activity below.**

1. Label the colonies with their correct names. Names that are too large may be put to the side with a line drawn to the colony being labeled.

2. Use the following symbols to show the major areas in which the following religious groups settled.

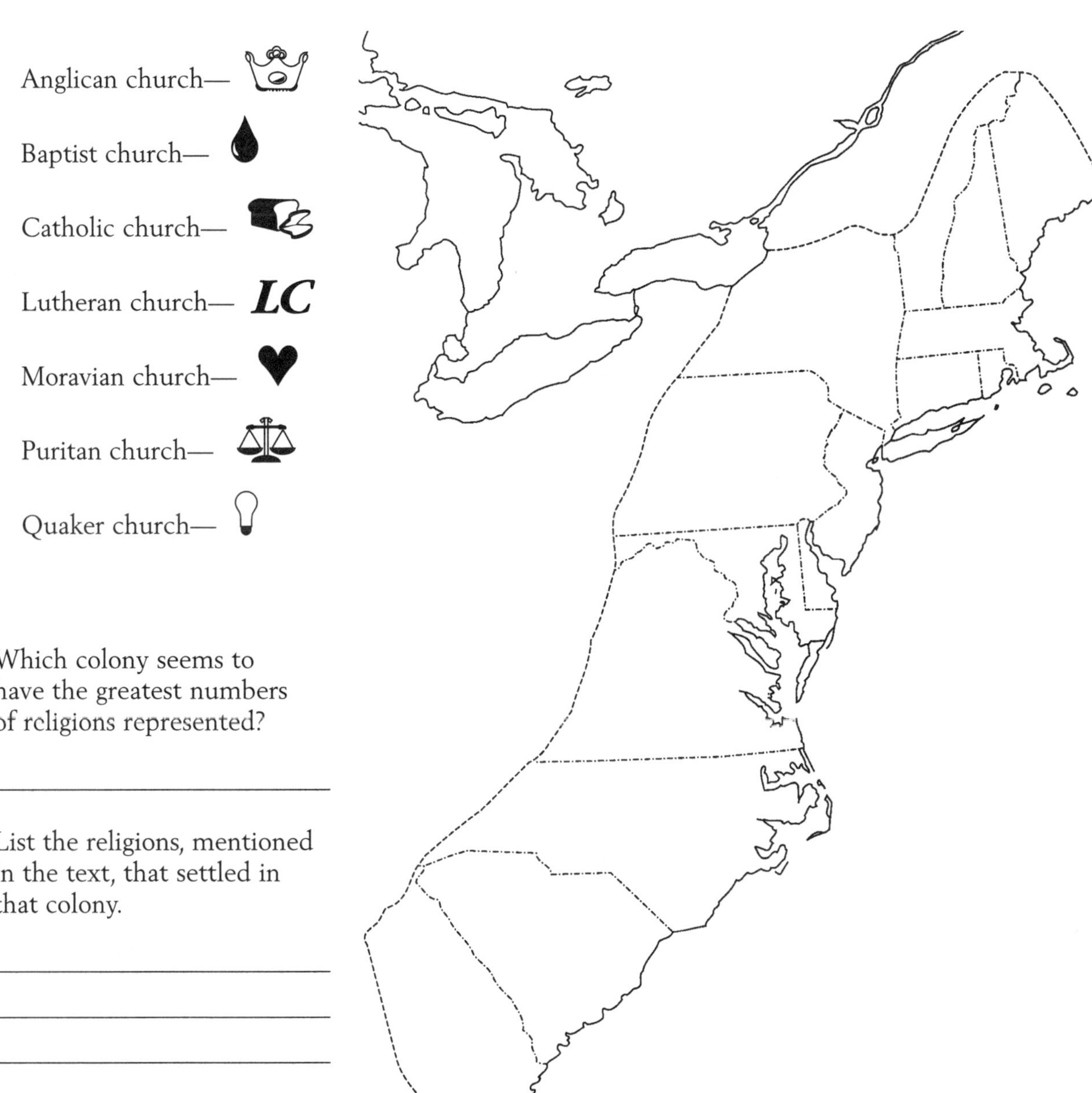


3. Which colony seems to have the greatest numbers of religions represented?

______________________

4. List the religions, mentioned in the text, that settled in that colony.

______________________

______________________

______________________

______________________

## Early Denominations and Their Leaders

**Match the denomination names with the phrase that best describes them.**

_______ 1. Puritan church that elected its own officers

_______ 2. allowed unconverted members to have full privileges of citizenship

_______ 3. guided by "Inner Light"; also called "Friends"

_______ 4. emphasized conversion and holy living

_______ 5. refused to serve in the military or to hold office

_______ 6. followers of John Huss; conducted much mission work

_______ 7. agreed with the Puritans but saw no problem in the Anglican church's ceremonies

_______ 8. emphasized doctrine of baptism by immersion

_______ 9. numerically the most important Anabaptists

_______ 10. believed Anglican system of church government was divinely ordained

_______ 11. followed teachings of Martin Luther

_______ 12. church members voted on ruling elders, who voted on the next level of church authority, etc.

_______ 13. more conservative Anabaptists; practiced strict church discipline

A. Amish
B. Anabaptists
C. Baptists
D. Congregationalists
E. Half-Way Covenant
F. high church Anglicans
G. low church Anglicans
H. Lutherans
I. Mennonites
J. Moravians
K. Pietists
L. Presbyterians
M. Quakers

**Match the preacher with his denomination.**

_______ 14. George Fox

_______ 15. Menno Simons

_______ 16. Roger Williams

_______ 17. Francis Makemie

_______ 18. Count Zinzendorf

_______ 19. Henry Mühlenberg

A. Baptist
B. Lutheran
C. Mennonite
D. Moravian
E. Presbyterian
F. Quaker

## Colonial Sunday

**Put words in the blanks that will correctly complete the paragraph.**

I just heard the (1) _____________ from the church, and mother and father are urging us out the door. It is so cold this November morning! As we enter the church, I look longingly at the (2) _____________ _____________ that the Hancock family bought. Oh, to be away from the drafts that swirl around inside the room. Our church was built just last summer; so it is very modern. Our pastor preaches from a (3) _____________ _____________ pulpit. He looks so majestic! The new (4) _____________ _____________ helps his voice carry to every corner of the church as he prays through the (5) _____________ _____________ _____________. Morning service goes quickly, and it is time for (6) _____________ class. My sister and I have practiced, and we know all the correct responses. After lunch we come back to afternoon services. I love to sing the psalms from the (7) _____________ _____________ _____________. My favorite is the (8) "_____________ _____________" based on Psalm 100. I look toward the (9) _____________ where the Hancocks' (10) _____________ sit. They had to get up there by a (11) _____________ on the outside of the church. When we sing, their voices sound like those of angels drifting down, mixing with the congregational voices as the (12) _____________ (13) "_____________ _____________" a hymn. The service grows long, and I flinch as the pastor flips over the (14) _____________ and continues reading his sermon. Poor Mr. Anders in the pew in front is falling asleep. Oh, oh! Here comes the (15) _____________ to give him a rap on the head. Seeing that, I know I will be wide awake the rest of the service.

## What Is Missing?

**Fill in the blanks with the correct answer.**

1. A school founded to train Indians but eventually opened to whites was ___________________ College.

2. The first Bible printed in America was in the ___________________ Indian language.

3. The Swedish Lutheran John ___________________ worked among the Delaware Indians.

4. Roger ___________________ was one of the first white men in New England to preach to the Indians.

5. John Eliot's converts formed communities called ___________________ villages.

6. Many congregationalists sadly mistook ___________________ for salvation and forced European standards on the Indians.

7. Although David Brainerd died young, his ___________________ inspired many young men to enter mission work.

8. One of the most successful Moravian missions, "Gnadenhutten," was directed by David ___________________.

9. Congregationalists and Moravians did extensive work in Indian___________________.

10. ___________________ ___________________ entered Yale before he was fourteen and was perhaps the greatest theologian of the Great Awakening.

11. The Great Awakening affected ___________________ and ___________________ life as well as religious.

12. ___________________ ___________________ was the Great Awakening's outstanding evangelist.

13. In New England the ___________________ ___________________ was slowly filling Congregational churches with unconverted members.

14. The Awakening was a breakthrough for ___________________ ___________________ because it reaffirmed the ___________________ ___________________ ___________________ ___________________ before God.

15. The Great Awakening was a powerful ___________________, ___________________, and ___________________ force that permanently altered the face of ___________________ ___________________.

## French and Indian Questions

**Write the answers to the questions in the blanks provided.**

1. What Ottawa Indian chief led a war against the British after the French and Indian War? _______________

2. What treaty brought an end to Queen Anne's War?

   _______________

3. What general tried to capture Fort Duquesne by organized, open battle?

   _______________

4. What is a method of warfare that uses sudden surprise attacks by small groups of hidden troops? _______________

5. What was Ben Franklin's plan to centralize the colonial rule?

   _______________

6. What treaty removed French influence as a major force in North America?

   _______________

7. What French Canadian leader caused great trouble for the English settlements in King William's War? _______________

8. What group did the British forcibly remove from Nova Scotia?

   _______________

9. Which talented soldier and engineer of defeats against the British was given command of French forces in America? _______________

10. In which battle near Quebec did the British rout the French, bringing an end to the war? _______________

11. Which prime minister of Great Britain developed a plan to win the war?

    _______________

12. Where did a large force of French soldiers and Indian warriors wait for Washington and his men? _______________

13. Which British commander was given the key campaign of the war?

    _______________

14. What powerful fortress in North America controlled the mouth of the St. Lawrence River? _______________

15. What was the key campaign of the war?

    _______________

## Map Study: French and Indian Wars

**Use the maps on pages 89, 94, and 95 of the text and an atlas to complete this map study. Some locations may need to be approximated.**

1. Label the following. Cities will be shown with dots; forts will be shown with solid triangles.

   Lakes—Erie, Ontario, and Champlain
   Rivers—Hudson, St. Lawrence, Mississippi, and Ohio
   Places—Albany, Boston, Montreal, New Orleans, Quebec, Nova Scotia
   Forts—Fort Detroit, Fort Duquesne, Fort Frontenac, Fort Michilimackinac, Fort Niagara, Fort William Henry

2. Color the following:

   Yellow—First location of the Acadians
   Red—Relocation site for many Acadians
   Black line—Around French holdings before Treaty of Paris
   Blue—Spanish portion of former French holdings
   Green—British portion of former French holdings

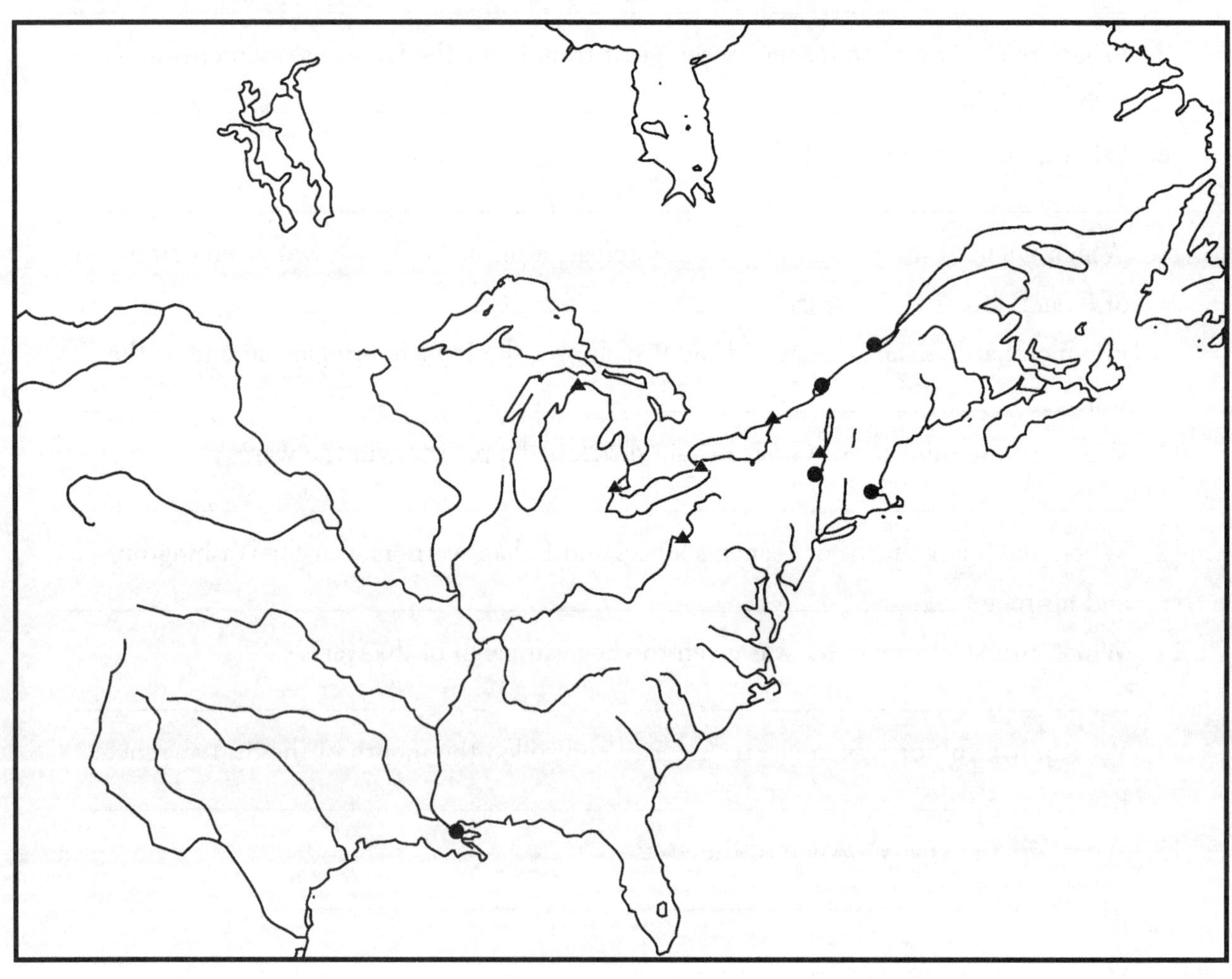

## Ordering

**Put the following lists in chronological order.**

| | |
|---|---|
| French and Indian War | 1. ____________________ |
| King George's War | 2. ____________________ |
| King William's War | 3. ____________________ |
| Pontiac's War | 4. ____________________ |
| Queen Anne's War | 5. ____________________ |
| Treaty of Paris | 6. ____________________ |
| Treaty of Utrecht | 7. ____________________ |
| | |
| Proclamation Line | 8. ____________________ |
| Quartering Act | 9. ____________________ |
| Townshend Acts | 10. ____________________ |
| Stamp Act | 11. ____________________ |
| Sugar Act | 12. ____________________ |

**Describe the five parliamentary decisions above and tell how they affected the colonists.**

13. ________________________________________________

________________________________________________

________________________________________________

14. ________________________________________________

________________________________________________

________________________________________________

15. ________________________________________________

________________________________________________

________________________________________________

16. ________________________________________________

________________________________________________

________________________________________________

17. ________________________________________________

________________________________________________

________________________________________________

## Crossword Puzzle

### Across

1. fort at the Forks of the Ohio
6. a French padre who paddled far down the Mississippi
9. French territory later given to Spain
14. queen after whom a war was named
16. led French Canadians during King William's War
18. site of the battle for Quebec
20. British prime minister with a plan
21. cut a road for his troops but was killed in the battle
22. tax on goods produced and consumed in the colonies
23. British minister intent on balancing the books
24. claimed Louisiana for France
25. site of a congress promoting colonial unity
26. half of a French explorer duo

### Down

2. French Canadian capital
3. taxed along with molasses and coffee
4. took Louisbourg and Quebec for the British
5. Virginia colonel who surrendered Fort Necessity
6. French commander in French and Indian War
7. law subjecting colonies to a standing army in peace
8. important power to be held by colonial assemblies
10. "first blood" of the Revolution
11. His "Acts" brought angry reactions.
12. "the War" that ended in 1763
13. the "Farmer in Pennsylvania"
15. forbade settlement beyond Appalachians
17. declared, "Give me liberty, or give me death!"
18. 1763 treaty that changed the face of North America
19. proposed the Albany Plan

## Explosive Events

**Fill in the bursts with the events that are recorded on pages 106-9 of the text.**

### American Action

1. 

Committee of Correspondence formed

3. 

Continental Congress

5. 

### British Action

British court of inquiry established—"purse strings" taken

2. 

Coercive Acts & Quebec Act

4. 

Gage goes to Concord to seize munitions stockpile.

6.

## Conflict Conclusions

**Evaluate the following events and battles covered on pages 115-22 of the text. Tell whether each one helped or hurt the American cause by checking the appropriate box, and then defend your viewpoint in the blanks provided.**

Helped
Hurt

☐ ☐ 1. Battle of Long Island ___________________________

___________________________

___________________________

___________________________

___________________________

☐ ☐ 2. Sea battle of the *Bonhomme Richard* and *Serapis* ___________________________

___________________________

___________________________

___________________________

___________________________

☐ ☐ 3. Attack on Trenton ___________________________

___________________________

___________________________

___________________________

___________________________

☐ ☐ 4. Battle of Brandywine ___________________________

___________________________

___________________________

___________________________

___________________________

☐ ☐ 5. Battle of Monmouth ___________________________

___________________________

___________________________

___________________________

___________________________

## Map Study: The Revolution

**Refer to the text, the maps on pages 111, 118, 123, and 124 of the text, and an atlas to complete this study.**

1. Label the following locations. Battle locations are marked with a star; forts are marked with a solid triangle; and other locations are marked with a dot. Trace the rivers with blue colored pencil and label them.

| | | | |
|---|---|---|---|
| Augusta | Bennington | Brandywine | Bunker Hill |
| Camden | Charleston | Concord | Cowpens |
| Delaware River | Fort Moultrie | Fort Ticonderoga | Guilford Court House |
| Hudson River | Kings Mountain | Lake Champlain | Lexington |
| Long Island | Monmouth | New York City | Philadelphia |
| Princeton | Saratoga | Trenton | Valley Forge |
| West Point | Wilmington, N.C. | Yorktown | |

2. Complete the following chart dealing with the major battles. (Use *B* for British and *A* for American.)

| Battle | Date | Who won | Colony | Commanders B/A |
|---|---|---|---|---|
| Bunker Hill | June 16, 1775 | B | Massachusetts | Gage/unnamed |
| | | | | |
| | | | | |
| | | | | |
| | | | | |
| | | | | |

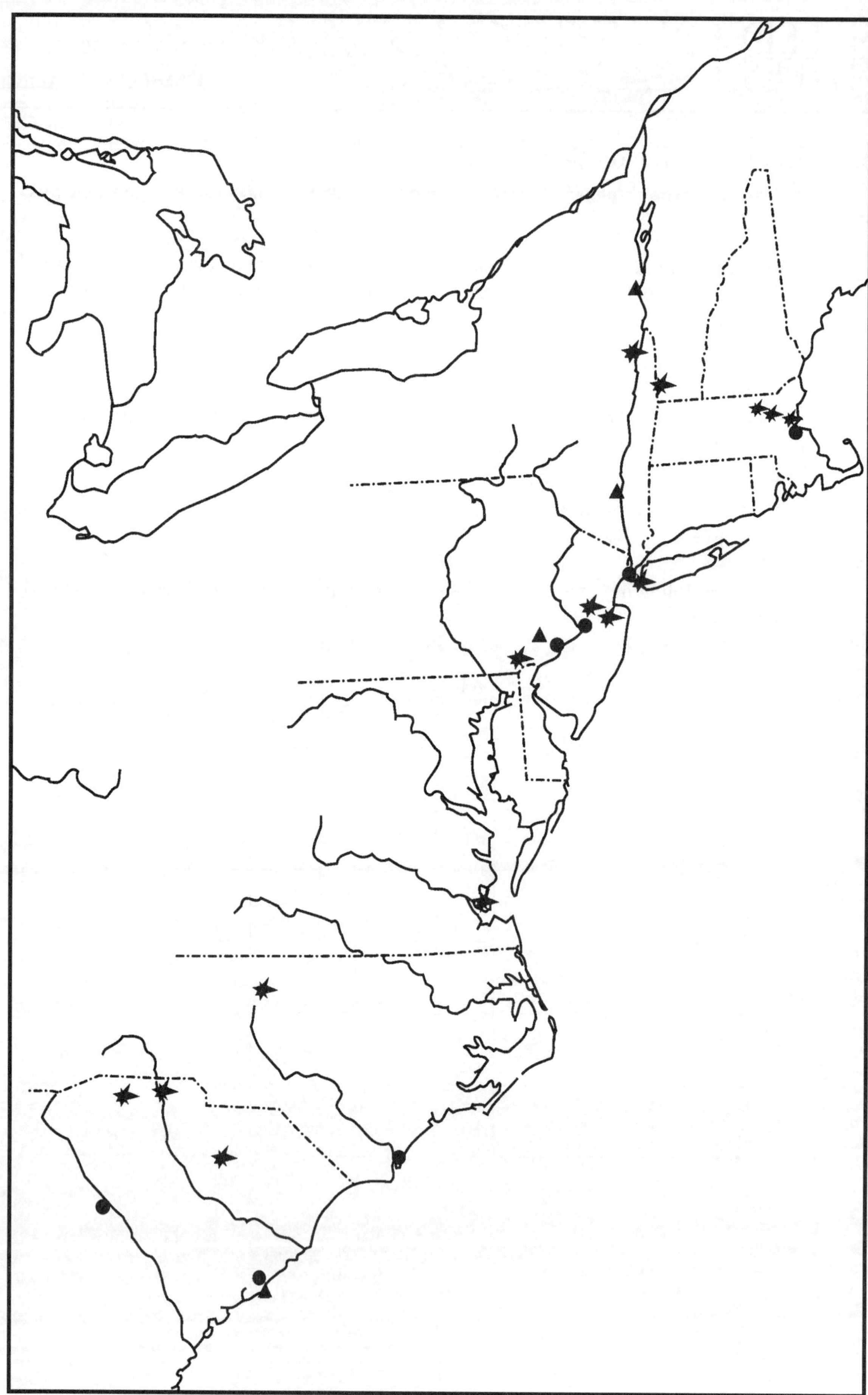

## Military Melee

**Put the correct letter in the blank provided.**

_______ 1. Cornwallis's Waterloo

_______ 2. captured Vincennes with a force of 150 men

_______ 3. the author of *Common Sense*

_______ 4. forced the British to evacuate Boston

_______ 5. the main author of the Declaration of Independence

_______ 6. professional soldiers

_______ 7. Molly Pitcher became a legend in this battle.

_______ 8. British general who surrendered Fort Ticonderoga

_______ 9. commanded the "Green Mountain Boys"

_______ 10. citizen soldiers

_______ 11. British-paid German soldiers

_______ 12. whom Tarleton said "the devil himself could not catch"

_______ 13. won the Battle of Long Island

_______ 14. Americans who fought for independence

_______ 15. German drillmaster for the Continental army

_______ 16. document that pledged loyalty to the king

_______ 17. Loyalists

_______ 18. the turning point of the war

_______ 19. brilliant soldier turned traitor

_______ 20. Washington's famous crossing of the Delaware was to get to this.

A. Baron von Steuben
B. Benedict Arnold
C. Ethan Allen
D. George Rogers Clark
E. Francis Marion
F. Henry Knox
G. Hessians
H. John Burgoyne
I. Yorktown
J. militia
K. Monmouth
L. Olive Branch Petition
M. Patriots
N. regulars
O. Saratoga campaign
P. Thomas Jefferson
Q. Thomas Paine
R. Tories
S. Trenton
T. William Howe

## Treaty of Paris, 1783

**Summarize the following articles agreed to by the United States and Great Britain in the Treaty of Paris, 1783.**

Article 1: His Brittanic Majesty acknowledges the said United States, viz., New Hampshire, Massachusetts Bay, Rhode Island and Providence Plantations, Connecticut, New York, New Jersey, Pennsylvania, Maryland, Virginia, North Carolina, South Carolina and Georgia, to be free sovereign and independent states, that he treats with them as such, and for himself, his heirs, and successors relinquishes all claims to the government, property, and territorial rights of the same and every part thereof.

_________________________________________________

_________________________________________________

_________________________________________________

Article 4: It is agreed that creditors on either side shall meet with no lawful impediment to the recovery of the full value in sterling money of all bona fide debts heretofore contracted.

_________________________________________________

_________________________________________________

_________________________________________________

Article 8: The navigation of the river Mississippi, from its source to the ocean, shall forever remain free and open to the subjects of Great Britain and the citizens of the United States.

_________________________________________________

_________________________________________________

_________________________________________________

Article 10: The solemn ratifications of the present treaty expedited in good and due form shall be exchanged between the contracting parties in the space of six months or sooner, if possible, to be computed from the day of the signatures of the present treaty. In witness whereof we the undersigned, their ministers plenipotentiary, have in their name and in virtue of our full powers, signed with our hands the present definitive treaty and caused the seals of our arms to be affixed thereto.

_________________________________________________

_________________________________________________

_________________________________________________

## Map Study: Northwest Territory

**Refer to the maps on pages x-xi, 136, and 138 and to the Appendix on page 658.**

1. Label the following boundaries of the Northwest Territory:

   The Great Lakes—Erie, Huron, Ontario, Michigan, and Superior
   The Mississippi and Ohio Rivers

2. Label the thirteen original states and the dates of their entrance into the Union.

3. Highlight in green the boundary of the Northwest Territory and color the territory itself yellow.

4. Label in black the states that would later be formed in the territory and the dates of their entrance into the Union.

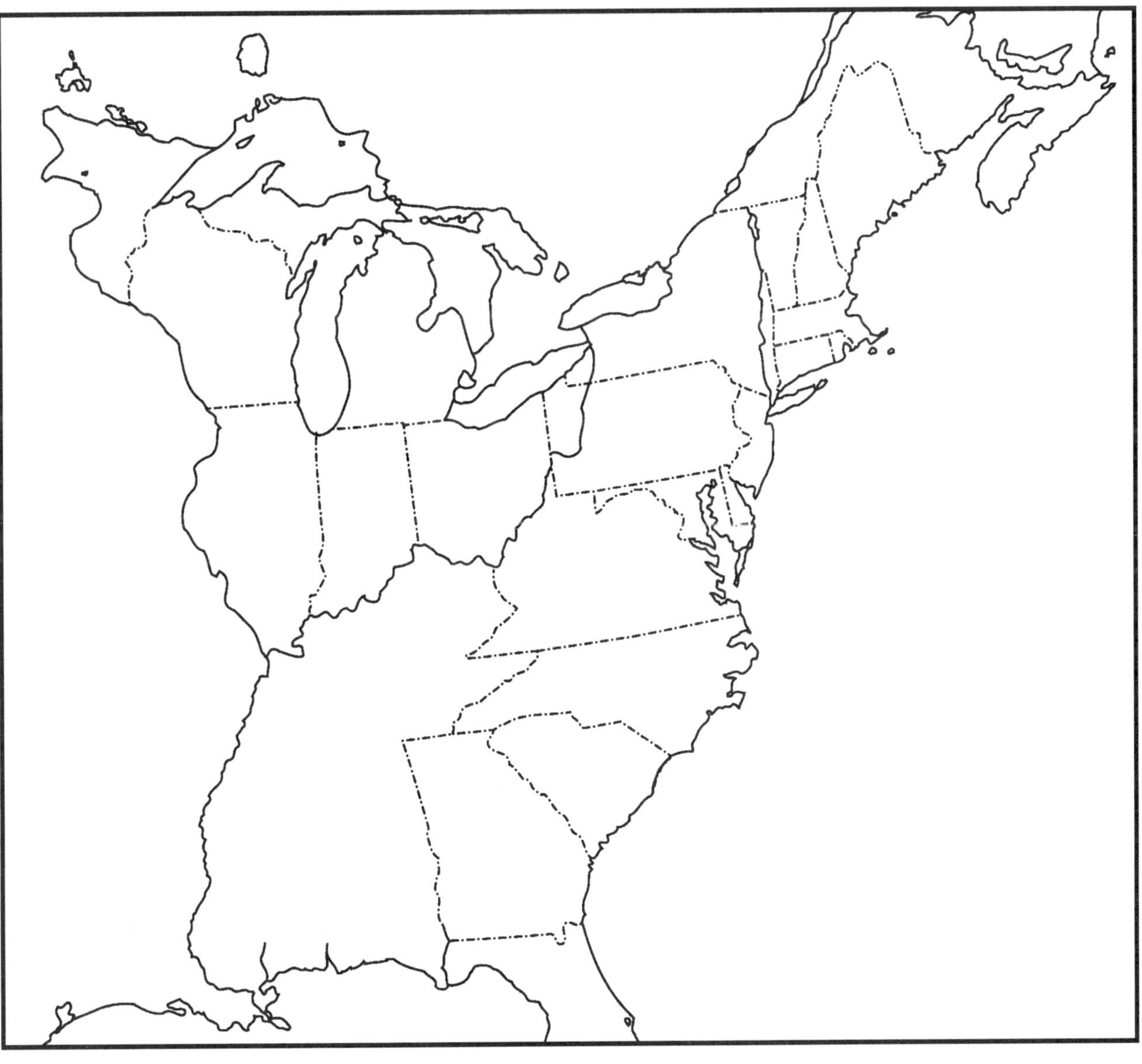

## Separate Powers

**Find two news articles that illustrate how any one of the three branches of government is currently exercising its powers. Answer the following questions about each article. If the article refers to two branches of government, you should choose one branch.**

### ARTICLE I

1. What branch of government is involved in the article?

   ___________________________________________________________

2. What is the constitutional power granted to that branch?

   ___________________________________________________________

3. How does it exercise its constitutional power?

   ___________________________________________________________

   ___________________________________________________________

   ___________________________________________________________

4. Does its action result in a check or balance on another branch of government? If so, how?

   ___________________________________________________________

   ___________________________________________________________

   ___________________________________________________________

   ___________________________________________________________

### ARTICLE II

1. What branch of government is involved in the article?

   ___________________________________________________________

2. What is the constitutional power granted to that branch?

   ___________________________________________________________

3. How does it exercise its constitutional power?

   ___________________________________________________________

   ___________________________________________________________

   ___________________________________________________________

4. Does its action result in a check or balance on another branch of government? If so, how?

   ___________________________________________________________

   ___________________________________________________________

   ___________________________________________________________

   ___________________________________________________________

# Who Am I?

**Read each statement and decide who would have said it. Write the correct answer in the blank.**

_______________________ 1. I was a Massachusetts farmer who tried to close the courts in the western part of the state.

_______________________ 2. I had a plan for dividing the Northwest Territory into ten states with names like "Cherronesus."

_______________________ 3. I wrote under the pen name "Publius."

_______________________ 4. I led the Anti-Federalists of Virginia with my fiery oratory.

_______________________ 5. I read a letter and stopped a conspiracy.

_______________________ 6. I was called the "Father of the Constitution."

_______________________ 7. I used the pen name "Cato" to denounce the Constitution.

_______________________ 8. I was the first vice president of the United States.

_______________________ 9. I had often wondered whether it was a rising or a setting sun painted behind the president's chair; I was happy to know it was a rising sun.

_______________________ 10. My compromise saved the Constitutional Convention and the Constitution.

_______________________ 11. Because it failed to guarantee civil liberties, I said that I "would sooner chop off [my] right hand" than sign the final draft of the Constitution.

_______________________ 12. I headed the committee that wrote the Articles of Confederation.

_______________________ 13. As president of the Congress in 1776, I was the first person to sign the Declaration of Independence.

_______________________ 14. I said that I doubted "whether one single law of any lawgiver, ancient or modern, has produced effects of more distinct, marked, and lasting character than the ordinance of '87."

## What's the Question?

**Just what you've wanted, an assignment with all the answers. Now write questions to fit.**

1. a close alliance of states ______________________

2. changes or additions (to the Constitution) ______________________

3. having one house (congress) ______________________

4. having two houses (congress) ______________________

5. The new lands were divided into townships of thirty-six sections or lots of one square mile. ______________________

6. May 25, 1787 ______________________

7. This plan wanted two houses with representation based on state population. ______________________

8. This plan wanted one house with each state having one vote. ______________________

9. the Great Compromise, or Connecticut Compromise ______________________

10. They wanted their back pay, and some wanted to establish a new government under a king. ______________________

11. United States government paper money ______________________

12. limited government ______________________

13. the Three-Fifths Compromise ______________________

14. the electoral college ______________________

15. April 30, 1789 ______________________

16. "Rogue Island" ______________________

17. federalism ______________________

18. gold or silver used as money ______________________

19. checks and balances ______________________

20. popular sovereignty ______________________

## Cabinet Confusion

**Compare the growth of government by listing the offices in both Washington's cabinet and today's cabinet. Write the dates that today's cabinet positions were first established. Use your book and an almanac.**

### Washington's Cabinet

_______________________________

_______________________________

_______________________________

### Today's Cabinet          Date Established

_______________________________          _______________________

_______________________________          _______________________

_______________________________          _______________________

_______________________________          _______________________

_______________________________          _______________________

_______________________________          _______________________

_______________________________          _______________________

_______________________________          _______________________

_______________________________          _______________________

_______________________________          _______________________

_______________________________          _______________________

_______________________________          _______________________

_______________________________          _______________________

1. What does the number of departments in the cabinet say about the power of the

   federal government today? ___________________________________________

   ___________________________________________________________________

   ___________________________________________________________________

2. Why do you think so many departments were formed or split in the past twenty-two

   years? _____________________________________________________________

   ___________________________________________________________________

   ___________________________________________________________________

## The Second President of the United States
**Use the textbook to finish the narrative.**

My name is (1) _________________ _________________, and I am the second president of the United States. Much of what has affected my term of office took place during Washington's second term. In 1793, the British began attacking our ships. We thought that (2) _________________ _________________ would solve the problem, but it only caused (3) _________________ to become more hostile. They began raiding so many of our ships that we became embroiled in what was called a (4) _________________ _________________; not formally declared war, but a conflict nonetheless. The French thought that we were so desperate for it to end that they sent agents to demand money from us to stop their raids. We refused, of course. Later, when Congress asked to see the correspondence regarding the affair, I dared not use the agents' real names; so it became known as the (5) _________________ _________________. When the opportunity came to make peace, my political party, the (6) _________________, were against me. To preserve my country meant losing their support. When the conflict ended with an anti-French sentiment in the colonies, it was easy for the Federalist Congress to propose the series of acts called the (7) _________________ and _________________ Acts. The first act placed restrictions on immigrants and gave me much more power to imprison undesirables. The second act went too far, however, when it made it illegal to speak or write certain things against the government or the president. My opponents Jefferson and Madison were quick to respond with their (8) _________________ and _________________ Resolutions respectively. Urging his supporters to make their views known by the ballot, (9) _________________ made his bid for the presidency well known. The decisions I made in office I made for my countrymen, but in doing so I lost their support. Even as the inauguration of the third president of the United States takes place today, I leave office knowing that my (10) _________________ _________________ will at least keep the Federalists in power in the judiciary.

## False Impressions

**Correctly identify the statement as true or false by circling the appropriate letter. If the statement is false, correct it to make it true.**

T   F   1.  The first ten amendments to the Constitution were called the Judiciary Act of 1789.

______________________________________________________________

T   F   2.  In an effort to quiet political opposition, the Federalist-controlled Congress passed the Alien and Sedition Acts.

______________________________________________________________

T   F   3.  President Adams had "midnight appointments" with congressmen to try to influence their decisions.

______________________________________________________________

T   F   4.  Adams and Jefferson remained bitter enemies till their deaths.

______________________________________________________________

T   F   5.  Because of taxation on liquor production, backcountry Pennsylvania farmers rose up in what was called the Whiskey Rebellion.

______________________________________________________________

T   F   6.  Citizen Genêt tried to stir up pro-French feelings to persuade America to side with France against Britain.

______________________________________________________________

T   F   7.  The Jay Treaty achieved one great result; it averted war with France.

______________________________________________________________

T   F   8.  Washington appointed four men as an advisory group that later became known as the cabinet.

______________________________________________________________

T   F   9.  Thomas Jefferson proposed a bill and later persuaded Washington to sign it, creating the first National Bank.

______________________________________________________________

T   F  10.  Congress members who wanted more flexibility interpreting the Constitution on certain issues were called loose constructionists.

______________________________________________________________

T   F  11.  Hamilton's *Report on Public Credit* caused a stir that ended with the present site of the capital of the United States being chosen.

______________________________________________________________

T   F  12.  President Washington issued a Proclamation of Neutrality to avoid involvement in the clashes between Canada and Britain.

______________________________________________________________

## Early Political Parties

**As the early political parties emerged, they had some sharp differences. Draw an *X* in the column of the party to which the center phrase or word applies and briefly explain how it applies.**

| *FEDERALIST* | | *REPUBLICAN* |
|---|---|---|
| | Jefferson and Burr | |
| | Future lay in commerce | |
| | Jeffersonians | |
| | True keepers of the Constitution | |
| | Pro-French trade | |
| | Adams and Pinckney | |
| | Hamiltonians | |
| | Future lay in farms | |
| | Last line of defense against tyranny | |
| | Pro-British trade | |
| | Monarchists | |

## Explore It Further

**Your text gives a brief account of the Lewis and Clark expedition. Use biographies or encyclopedias to answer the following questions and to fill out the map on the next page.**

1. What president of the United States commissioned the expedition? ________________

2. What was the full name of the man who was in charge of the Lewis and Clark expedition? ________________

3. What was the full name of his fellow explorer? ________________

4. What was their difference in rank? ________________

5. When and from where did they embark on their journey? ________________

6. What was the name of the slave that accompanied Clark? ________________

7. When and where did the one and only fatality of the expedition occur? ________________
________________

8. Who died and how? ________________

9. Who were the first hostile Indians encountered? ________________

10. Where were they confronted? ________________

11. What new animal did the expeditioners discover that they first described as a "barking squirrel"? ________________

12. What especially ferocious animal did the explorers encounter? ________________

13. Lewis took a pet on the expedition with him. Its name was Shannon. What was it? ________________ What breed? ________________

14. Where did the explorers spend their first winter? ________________

15. What Indian tribe did they name their fort after? ________________

16. What was the name of the Indian woman who went with the expedition? ________________

17. What tribe was she from? ________________

18. In what present-day state did they find the waterfalls that they encountered on the Missouri River? ________________ What are they called? ________________

19. Where did the explorers cross the continental divide? ________________

20. What river did Lewis name after his cousin Maria? ________________

21. When did they sight the Pacific Ocean? ________________

22. What was the name of the camp in Oregon they established to winter in? ________________

23. Why was Captain Lewis shot? ________________

24. On the return home, the party divided for a while to explore different routes. Which way did Lewis's division go? ________________

25. Which way did Clark's half go? ________________

26. On what date did they arrive back in St. Louis? ________________

## Map Study: Lewis and Clark Expedition

**Complete the map using the sources that you used to answer the questions on the previous page.**

1. Label the following places. The states named were not yet established.

   Rivers—Bad River, Columbia River, Marias River, Mississippi River, Missouri River, Snake River, Yellowstone River

   States—Idaho, Iowa, Kansas, Missouri, Montana, Nebraska, North and South Dakota, Oregon, Washington, Wyoming

   Cities—Bismarck, North Dakota; St. Louis, Missouri; Sioux City, Iowa

   Places—Cascade Range, Bitterroot Mountains, Pacific Ocean, Rocky Mountains

2. Place the proper symbols on the map to show the landmarks listed below.

   Fort Mandan—light flag
   Sgt. Floyd's grave—cross
   Lemhi Pass—light star
   Teton Sioux meeting—tomahawk

   Great Falls—drop of water
   Lolo Pass—dark star
   Fort Clatsop—dark flag

3. Draw with a black marker the route west that the expedition took.

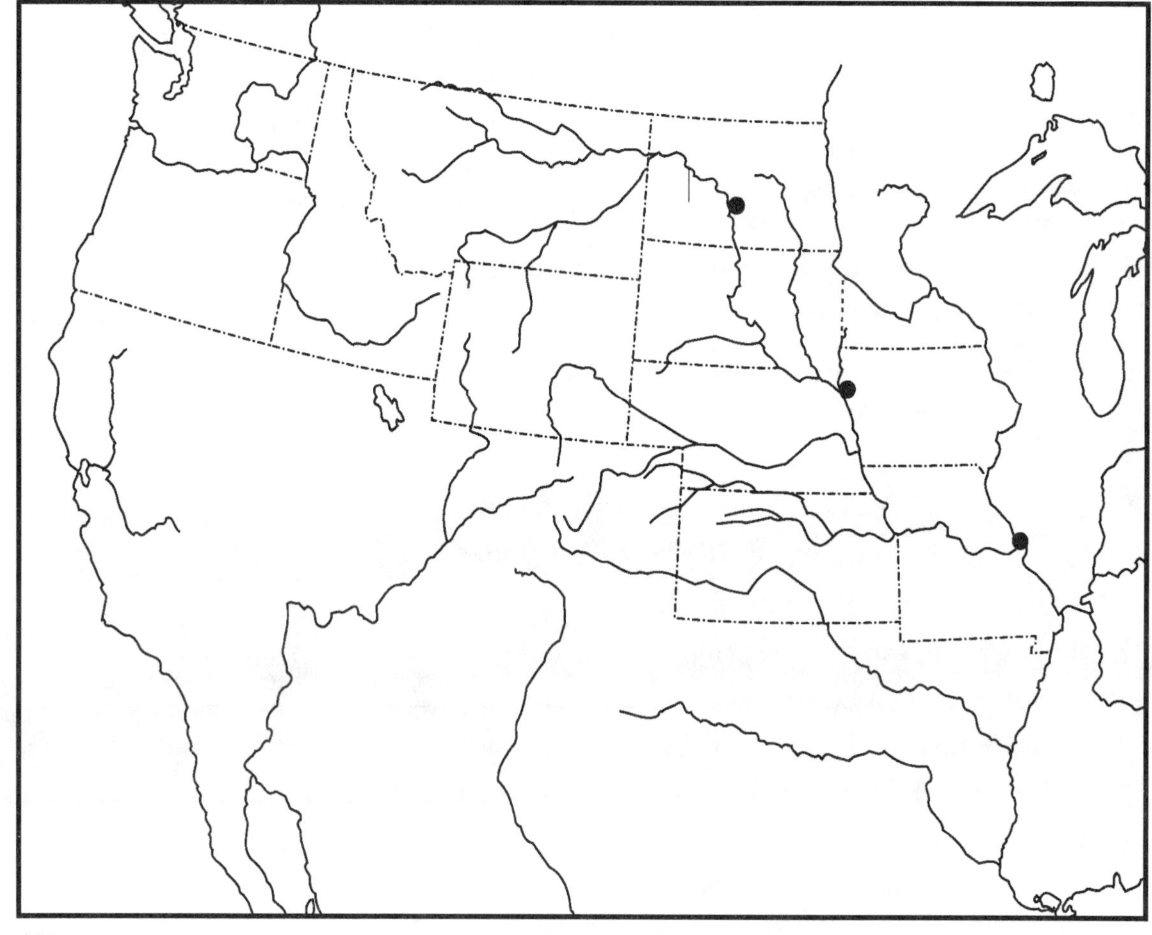

## Questions and Profiles

**Complete the following.**

**A. Answer the following questions.**

1. Which Revolutionary hero did Washington appoint to crush early Indian uprisings?

   ________________________________________________

2. Which Indian claimed to have received a revelation from the "Master of Life"?

   ________________________________________________

3. In which battle did the Indians think that the white man's weapons were charmed
   and, therefore, could not harm them? ________________________________________________

4. What was the trouble with treaties between the Americans and the Indians?

   ________________________________________________

   ________________________________________________

5. Which battle got its name because the fighting took place among trees knocked down
   by a storm? ________________________________________________

6. Which natural event was used by an influential Indian to support his claims of super-
   natural power? ________________________________________________

7. Which treaty opened the southern half of Ohio to settlers? ________________________________

8. In the Battle of the Thames, which general routed British and Indian forces?

   ________________________________________________

9. Which great Indian leader dreamed of an Indian confederation whose power could
   withstand the threat of the white man's takeover? ________________________________________

**B. Write a brief profile of the following using information from the textbook.**

1. Harrison—________________________________________________

   ________________________________________________

   ________________________________________________

   ________________________________________________

   ________________________________________________

2. Tecumseh—________________________________________________

   ________________________________________________

   ________________________________________________

   ________________________________________________

   ________________________________________________

## Map Study: The War of 1812

**To complete this activity, refer to the map on page 185 of the text.**

1. Label the new states that had joined the Union by 1812. Below each name, write the year in which the state was accepted into the Union. Refer to the Appendix on page 658.

   Vermont, Kentucky, Tennessee, Ohio, Louisiana

2. Label with a triangle Fort Dearborn, Fort McHenry, and Fort Niagara.

3. Label the five Great Lakes.

4. Label with a star the following War of 1812 battle locations.

   Bladensburg; Lake Erie; the Thames; York; Lake Champlain; Washington, D.C.; New Orleans; Horseshoe Bend

# The
# Capitol Gazette
## War of 1812 Prospectus

### Intimations of War

In looking back, it seems that the British were bent on generating hostilities with the United States. Their total disregard for the citizenship of our people was displayed in the random (1) ________________ of our seamen into British service. Of course, the (2) ________________ affair almost brought about the war in 1807. The American people were incensed that the captain of the British ship (3) ________________ would kill and take Americans. If it weren't for the fact that (4) ________________ persuaded Congress to ban all trade with the rest of the world in the (5) ________________, we would have gone to war immediately.

### Flying Toward Conflict

Congress soon found that those most hurt by the trade ban were not the British or French, but the (6) ________________. In the 1810 congressional elections, several prowar representatives joined the House. These intensely nationalistic men were called (7) ________________ and were headed by (8) ________________ of Kentucky and (9) ________________ of South Carolina. These men and their supporters began pressuring the United States president, (10) ________________,

to declare war on England. On (11) ________________, the president sent a war message to Congress. After heated debate, war was declared.

### On Land and at Sea

Little did the glorious British navy expect to have the upstart American navy win so many battles. One factor was the oak-sided American ship the (12) ________________, nicknamed (13) ________________. British cannonballs bounced right off. Another factor was the determination of the American captain (14) ________________, who built his own ships, dragged cannons through the wilderness to Lake Erie, and used sailors who had never been on anything larger than a flatboat. The British met defeat at his hands in the Battle of (15) ________________. In spite of victories in the Northwest Territory, the outlook was gloomy for the U.S. when Napoleon surrendered and England could turn all its attention to America. Against Tennessee general (16) ________________, the British suffered devastating defeat. Meanwhile, the (17) ________________ was signed in England. With that, the war was ended—a peace without victory.

## Headlines!

**Write news articles for two of the following headlines. Remember to include the important facts: who, what, when, where, why, and how. You may want to do extra research.**

Neutrality Impossible
War Hawks Gaining Ground
Tecumseh's Forces Narrowly Defeated

"Old Ironsides" Victorious
Attack on Fort McHenry Repulsed
"Old Hickory," the New Hero

*TITLE:* ___________________________________________

_______________________________________________________

_______________________________________________________

_______________________________________________________

_______________________________________________________

_______________________________________________________

_______________________________________________________

_______________________________________________________

_______________________________________________________

_______________________________________________________

_______________________________________________________

_______________________________________________________

*TITLE:* ___________________________________________

_______________________________________________________

_______________________________________________________

_______________________________________________________

_______________________________________________________

_______________________________________________________

_______________________________________________________

_______________________________________________________

_______________________________________________________

_______________________________________________________

_______________________________________________________

_______________________________________________________

_______________________________________________________

## Map Study: The Missouri Compromise

**Refer to page 196 of the text to complete this map.**

1. With red pencil, draw and label the Missouri Compromise line (36° 30').

2. Label all the states that were in the Union by 1821.

3. At the bottom left of the map, make a color key to identify the following areas and then color those areas according to your key.

Free states                    Slave states
Free territory                 Slave territory

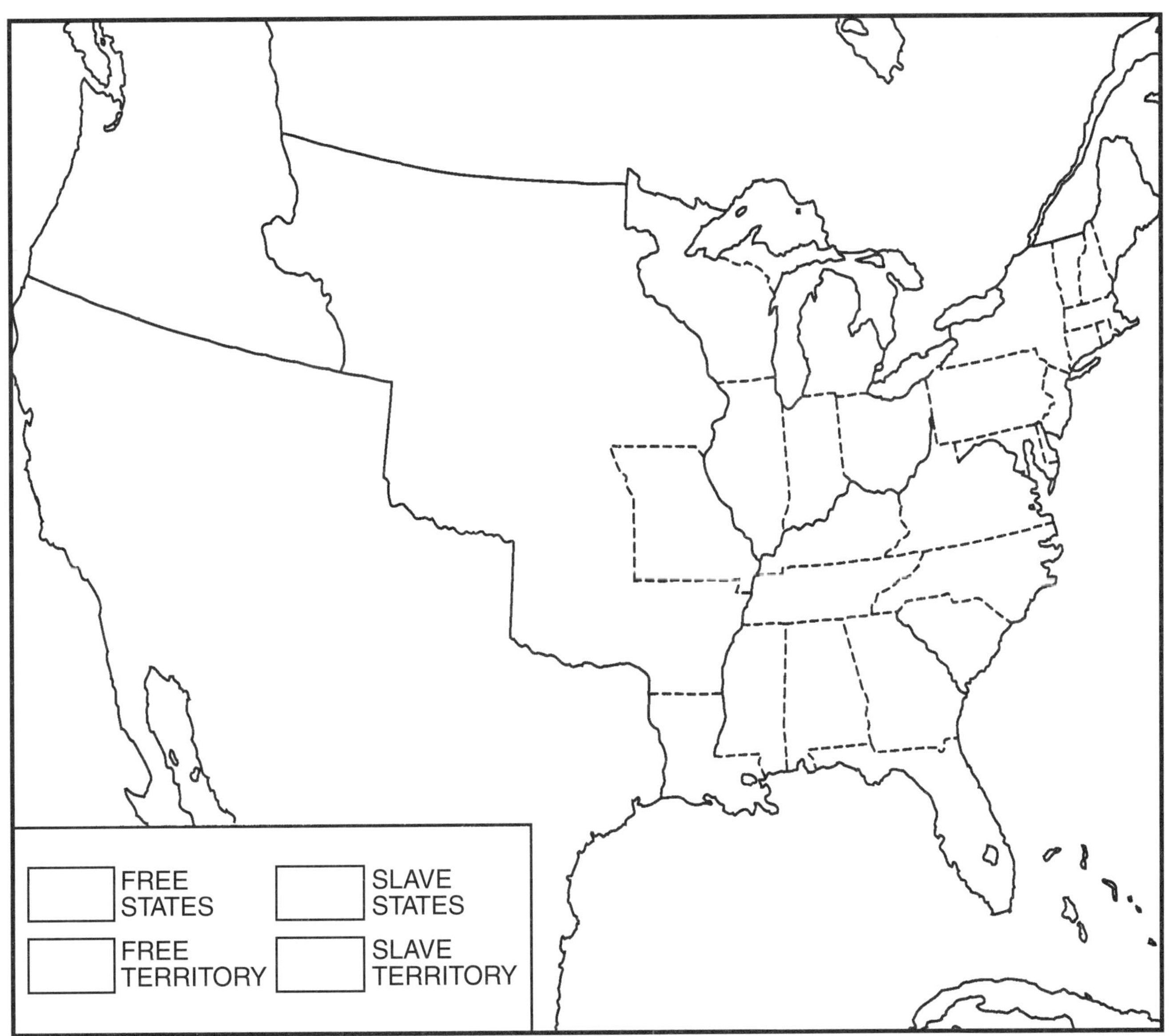

## Time Travels

**Put the letter for the correct date next to the event listed. Dates may be used more than once or not at all.**

________ 1. Harrison's death

________ 2. Jackson's first election

________ 3. completion of the National Road

________ 4. last caucus nomination

________ 5. Missouri Compromise

________ 6. first protective tariff

________ 7. John Q. Adams's election

________ 8. first tariff nullified by the South

________ 9. Clay's Compromise Tariff

________ 10. Jackson's second election

________ 11. beginning of forced Cherokee march

________ 12. start of five-year depression

________ 13. start of Black Hawk War

________ 14. order to use "specie" for land

________ 15. beginning of the Seminole War

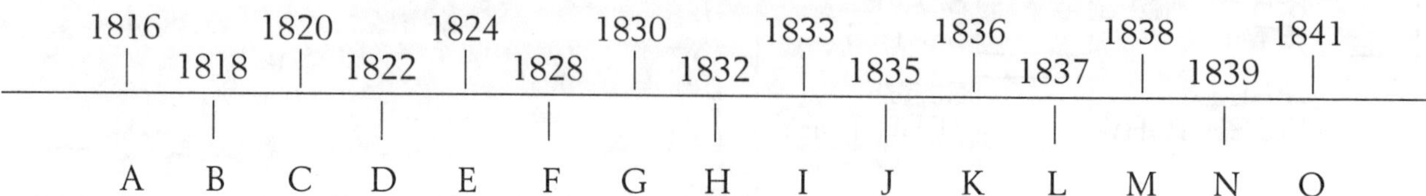

## Presidential Powers

**Put the letter of the correct answer in the blank provided.**

_______ 1. closed meeting to select candidates

_______ 2. accusation made against Adams and Clay

_______ 3. clubs that supported Van Buren

_______ 4. Cherokees' forced march to Oklahoma

_______ 5. Jackson's real advisors

_______ 6. Andrew Jackson

_______ 7. higher protective import tax of 1828

_______ 8. Martin Van Buren

_______ 9. state institutions used for federal deposits

_______ 10. caused by cotton price drop and irresponsible bank action

_______ 11. campaign cry for Harrison and his running mate

_______ 12. South Carolinian doctrine of rejecting unacceptable congressional acts as unconstitutional

_______ 13. presidential practice of replacing government officials with supporters

_______ 14. leader of Seminole Indians

_______ 15. prohibition of the use of anything but hard money for land purchase

_______ 16. economic collapse and five-year depression

_______ 17. the resolution which once again evened the political balance of slave and free states

_______ 18. gave the president war powers against South Carolina

A. "corrupt bargain"
B. "King Caucus"
C. "Kitchen Cabinet"
D. "Little Magician"
E. nullification
F. "O.K."
G. Force Bill
H. Osceola
I. Panic of 1837
J. "pet banks"
K. Specie Circular of 1836
L. spoils system
M. "Tariff of Abominations"
N. "Tippecanoe and Tyler too"
O. Trail of Tears
P. Panic of 1819
Q. Missouri Compromise
R. "Old Hickory"

## Crossword Puzzle

### Across

1. Adams's wing of the Democratic-Republicans
3. Sauk and Fox leader who waged war
4. a challenging group against the two-party system
6. improvements promoted by the American system
7. great orator of the Senate who defended the Union
8. Old Hickory's close advisors in the White House
12. high tariff of 1828
13. an internal improvement ending in Vandalia, Illinois
16. the other state admitted by the Missouri Compromise
17. Jackson's party
20. a depression such as the one in 1819
21. South Carolina senator who spoke up for secession
22. scarred by a sabre and shot in a duel
23. Van Buren's replacement for pet banks
24. Osceola's Indians

### Down

1. doctrine proposed by Calhoun
2. gathering of party delegates to nominate candidates
5. partisan replacement of officeholders
7. new anti-Jackson party
9. type of bargain allegedly made by Adams and Clay
10. tax on imported goods
11. type of banks in which Jackson placed federal deposits
14. Clay's economic nationalism; the "___ system"
15. a president, like his father
18. the "Little Magician"
19. closed nomination meeting of party leaders

## Map Study: The Growth of Transportation

**Refer to page 221 of the text to complete this map.**

1. Label the following places.

   Erie Canal, Chesapeake and Ohio Canal (C & O), Miami and Erie Canal (M & E), Ohio and Erie Canal, Wabash and Erie Canal, Lake Erie, Lake Michigan, Lake Ontario

2. Place a dot (•) with the city's name at the correct location for each of the following.

   Albany, Baltimore, Boonesboro, Buffalo, Cleveland, Evansville, Louisville, Natchez, New Orleans, Philadelphia, Richmond, Toledo, Vandalia

3. Draw and label the following: National Road, Natchez Trace, Wilderness Road.

## Think About It!

**It has been said, "Necessity is the mother of invention." Explain how the following inventions, transportation methods, and communication devices satisfied a need.**

| *Invention* | *Need* | *Previous Method* |
|---|---|---|
| Eli Whitney's interchangeable parts | 1. _______________ <br> _______________ <br> _______________ | _______________ <br> _______________ <br> _______________ |
| John Deere's steel-edged plow | 2. _______________ <br> _______________ <br> _______________ | _______________ <br> _______________ <br> _______________ |
| Eli Whitney's cotton gin | 3. _______________ <br> _______________ <br> _______________ | _______________ <br> _______________ <br> _______________ |
| Robert Fulton's steamship | 4. _______________ <br> _______________ <br> _______________ | _______________ <br> _______________ <br> _______________ |
| Governor Clinton's Erie Canal | 5. _______________ <br> _______________ <br> _______________ | _______________ <br> _______________ <br> _______________ |
| Samuel Morse's telegraph | 6. _______________ <br> _______________ <br> _______________ | _______________ <br> _______________ <br> _______________ |



## *Optional Activity*

**Define a need (other than social or moral) in today's society and design an invention to satisfy that need.**

## Who Am I?

**Read each statement and decide whom or what it best describes in art, architecture, or literature.**

_______________ 1. I was a "thorough democrat" who painted the common man.

_______________ 2. Although I spent most of my life in England, I greatly influenced and taught many American painters.

_______________ 3. I published many popular hymnbooks.

_______________ 4. As the master short-story writer of America, I wrote of the dark, tortured depths of man's soul.

_______________ 5. I dreamed of my wife, Jeanie, and wrote a ballad about my dream.

_______________ 6. I helped to develop the short story with works such as "Rip Van Winkle" and "The Legend of Sleepy Hollow."

_______________ 7. We used Greek revivalist architecture for the U.S. Capitol.

_______________

_______________ 8. In *Leaves of Grass*, I celebrated the glory and nobility of man.

_______________ 9. As a group, we specialized in portraying the beauty and serenity of America.

_______________ 10. I left a portrait unfinished, and it now appears on the one-dollar bill.

_______________ 11. In *Walden*, I wrote about my stay on Walden Pond.

_______________ 12. I wrote romantic views of the American frontier.

_______________ 13. This style of art duplicated the neoclassical style of Europe.

## Reform and Religion

**Using the textbook, fill in the following table.**

| Reform | Leader(s) | Changes Desired |
| --- | --- | --- |
| Abolition | | |
| | (no central leader given in the book) | Desired equal rights and suffrage for women |
| | Dorothea Dix | |
| Education | | |
| | (no central leader given in the book) | Desired a ban on sales and consumption of alcohol |
| Utopian reform | | |

### *Matching*

_______ 1. "New Measures"

_______ 2. Mormonism

_______ 3. "father of American Methodism"

_______ 4. African Methodist Episcopal Church bishop

_______ 5. originator of the camp meeting

_______ 6. set a date for Christ's return

_______ 7. supposed incarnation of God

_______ 8. primary creator of transcendentalism

_______ 9. preached messages that led to revival at Yale

_______ 10. greatest camp meeting held

_______ 11. first American mission board

_______ 12. series of religious services lasting several days

_______ 13. traveling from settlement to settlement in order to preach

_______ 14. first great hero of American missions

_______ 15. belief that God created the universe and then stood back and left it alone

A. ABCFM
B. Adoniram Judson
C. camp meeting
D. Cane Ridge, Kentucky
E. Charles Finney
F. circuit riding
G. deism
H. Francis Asbury
I. James McGready
J. Joseph Smith
K. Mother Ann Lee
L. Ralph Waldo Emerson
M. Richard Allen
N. Timothy Dwight
O. William Miller

## Remember the Alamo!

**Do some extra research in the library or with an encyclopedia at home. Look into the lives of three of the people listed below and answer the following questions about them.**

Jim Bowie, Davy Crockett, Santa Anna, William Travis

**Person 1** ___________________________

1. Where and when was he born? ___________________________________________

2. Who was his wife? ___________________________________________

3. How did he happen to be at the Alamo? ___________________________________________

___________________________________________

4. How did he contribute to the battle? ___________________________________________

___________________________________________

___________________________________________

5. What was the date of his death, and how old was he? ___________________________________________

___________________________________________

**Person 2** ___________________________

1. Where and when was he born? ___________________________________________

2. Who was his wife? ___________________________________________

3. How did he happen to be at the Alamo? ___________________________________________

___________________________________________

4. How did he contribute to the battle? ___________________________________________

___________________________________________

___________________________________________

5. What was the date of his death, and how old was he? ___________________________________________

___________________________________________

**Person 3** ___________________________

1. Where and when was he born? ___________________________________________

2. Who was his wife? ___________________________________________

3. How did he happen to be at the Alamo? ___________________________________________

___________________________________________

4. How did he contribute to the battle? ___________________________________________

___________________________________________

___________________________________________

5. What was the date of his death, and how old was he? ___________________________________________

___________________________________________

## From Sea to Shining Sea

**Use the text to fill in the table. Look back to previous chapters to find the information on Florida.**

| Territory | Prior Occupation | How Obtained | Date | New Boundaries |
|---|---|---|---|---|
| Texas | | Mexican/American War | | |
| Oregon | Britain/U.S. | treaty | | |
| Maine | | | 1842 | U.S. received 7/12 of disputed area |
| Florida | | | | Annexed entire peninsula |

Page 242 of the text quotes these words of John Louis O'Sullivan:

> Our manifest destiny [is] to overspread and to possess the whole of the continent which Providence has given us for the development of the great experiment of liberty and federated self-government entrusted to us.

Do you think this statement is correct? Defend your position.

_______________________________________________

_______________________________________________

_______________________________________________

_______________________________________________

_______________________________________________

_______________________________________________

_______________________________________________

_______________________________________________

_______________________________________________

_______________________________________________

_______________________________________________

_______________________________________________

_______________________________________________

## Mexican-American Relations

**Put the letter for the correct date next to the event.**

________ 1. Treaty of Guadalupe Hidalgo

________ 2. capture of Santa Fe

________ 3. first Texas settlement

________ 4. American troops first attacked by Mexican troops

________ 5. Battle of San Jacinto

________ 6. Bear Flag Republic established

________ 7. Scott's entrance into Vera Cruz

________ 8. Texas admitted to the Union

________ 9. Battle of Buena Vista

________ 10. declaration of war by Congress

________ 11. the battle at the Alamo

________ 12. Mexico City taken

________ 13. Taylor's assault on Monterrey

________ 14. election of President James K. Polk

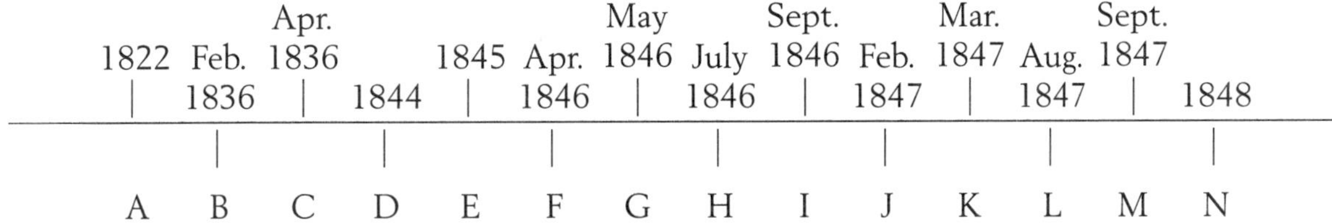

## Treaty of Guadalupe Hidalgo, 1848

**Summarize the following provisions agreed to by the United States and Mexico in the Treaty of Guadalupe Hidalgo.**

Article I: There shall be firm and universal peace between the United States of America and the Mexican Republic, and between their respective countries, territories, cities, towns, and people, without exception of places or persons.

Article I: _______________________________________________________________

_______________________________________________________________

Article XII: In consideration of the extension acquired by the boundaries of the United States, as defined in the fifth article of the present treaty, the Government of the United States engages to pay that of the Mexican Republic the sum of fifteen millions of dollars. . . .

Article XII: _______________________________________________________________

_______________________________________________________________

Article XVI: Each of the contracting parties reserves to itself the entire right to fortify whatever point within its territory it may judge proper so to fortify for its security.

Article XVI: _______________________________________________________________

_______________________________________________________________

Article XXI: If unhappily any disagreement should hereafter arise between the Governments of the two republics, whether with respect to the interpretation of any stipulation in this treaty, or with respect to any other particular concerning the political or commercial relations of the two nations, the said Governments, . . . do promise to each other that they will endeavour, . . . to settle the differences so arising, and to preserve the state of peace and friendship in which the two countries are now placing themselves, using, for this end, mutual representations and pacific negotiations. . . .

Article XXI: _______________________________________________________________

_______________________________________________________________

Article XXIII: This treaty shall be **ratified by the President of the United States of America, by and with the advice and consent of the Senate thereof;** and by the President of the Mexican Republic, with the previous approbation of its general Congress; . . . in four months from the date of the signature hereof, or sooner if practicable. . . .

Article XXIII: _______________________________________________________________

_______________________________________________________________

## Map Study: Manifest Destiny

**To complete the map on the next page, refer to the text and the maps on pages 242 and 252.**

1.  Put the following words or phrases under the heading that they best fit.

| Bear Flag Republic | cotton crop | Nueces River |
| 54° 40′ | lumberjacks | Marcus Whitman |
| Nez Perce Indians | iron ore | 49th parallel |
| Sacramento | Snake River | trappers |
| 12,000 mile argument | Sam Houston | John C. Frémont |
| cattle | | |

| **Oregon** | **California** | **Texas** | **Maine** |
|---|---|---|---|
| ____________ | ____________ | ____________ | ____________ |
| ____________ | ____________ | ____________ | ____________ |
| ____________ | ____________ | ____________ | ____________ |
| ____________ | ____________ | ____________ | ____________ |
| ____________ | ____________ | ____________ | ____________ |

2.  Label the following states and their dates of admission. (See the Appendix on page 658.)

    Indiana, Mississippi, Illinois, Alabama, Maine, Missouri, Arkansas, Michigan, Florida, Texas, Iowa, Wisconsin

3.  Label the following locations.

    Alamo, Missouri River, Mississippi River, Colorado River, Columbia River, Salt Lake City, Willamette River, Rio Grande, Sacramento, Santa Fe, Snake River, 49th parallel

4.  Label the following trails using the color indicated.

    Oregon Trail—blue, California Trail—red, Mormon Trail—green, Santa Fe Trail—yellow

5.  Use encyclopedias to help you draw in the boundaries for the following areas related to United States expansion. Shade the areas with different colored pencils and make a key to interpret your colors.

    Louisiana Purchase, Texas (including the disputed area), Gadsden Purchase, Mexican Cession

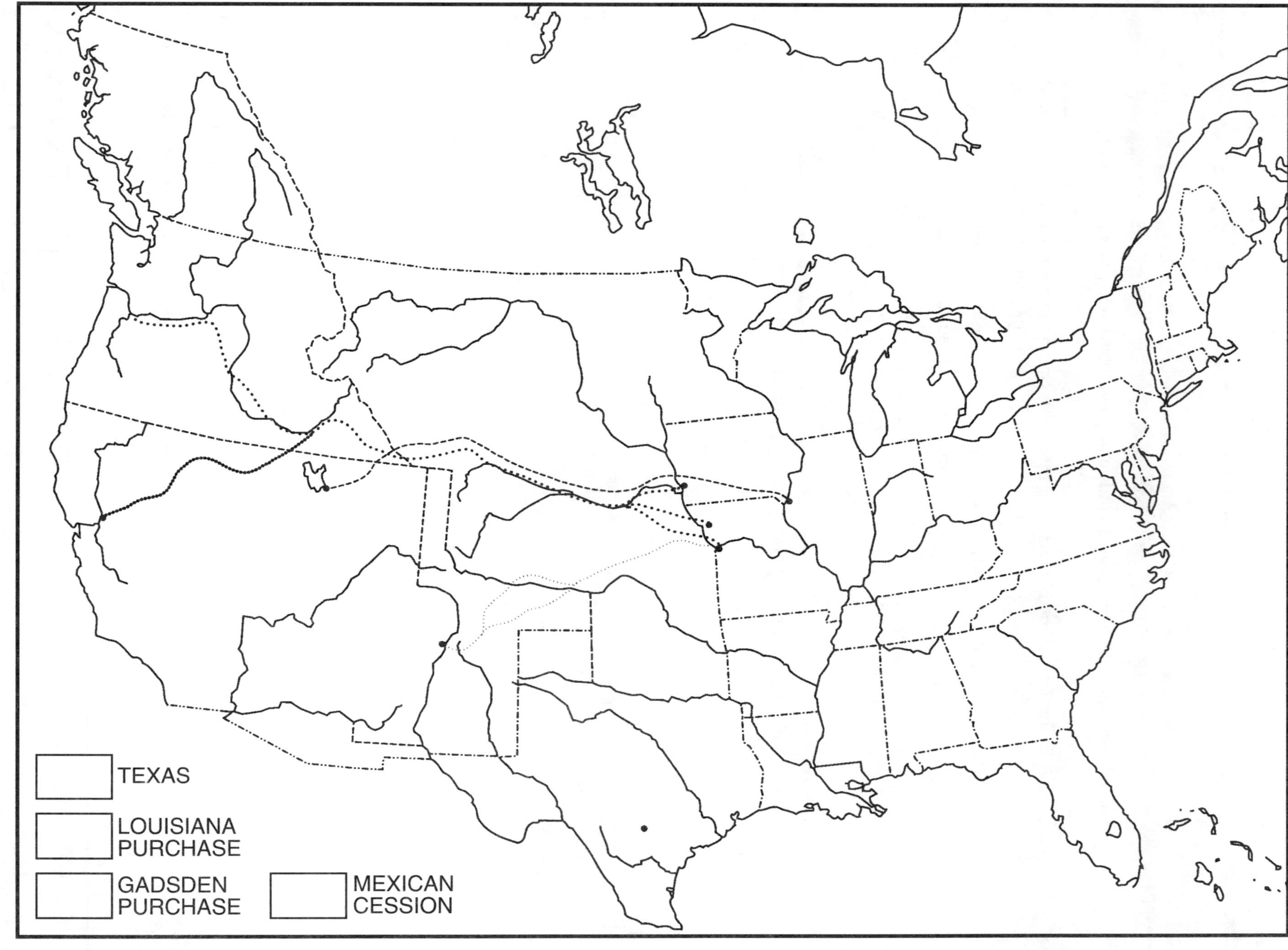

TEXAS
LOUISIANA PURCHASE
GADSDEN PURCHASE
MEXICAN CESSION

## Viewpoint

**Read and compare the following viewpoints on slavery and then answer the following questions on a separate sheet of paper.**

1. Which viewpoint do you think is least accurate? Why?
2. What biases did each writer bring into his account? How are they revealed?
3. Find five Bible verses that you think apply to slavery. Give the principle expressed in each verse and explain how it could have been applied to the slave question of the 1800s.

### Slave Viewpoint

The hands are required to be in the cotton field as soon as it is light in the morning and, with the exception of ten or fifteen minutes, which is given them at noon to swallow their allowance of cold bacon, they are not permitted to be a moment idle until it is too dark to see, and when the moon is full, they often times labor till the middle of the night. They do not dare to stop even at dinner time, not return to the quarters, however late it be, until the order to halt is given by the driver.

The day's work over in the field, the baskets are "toted," or, in other words, carried to the gin-house, where the cotton is weighed. No matter how fatigued and weary he may be—no matter how much he longs for sleep and rest—a slave never approaches the gin-house with his basket of cotton but with fear. If it falls short in weight—if he has not performed the full task appointed him, he knows that he must suffer. And if he has exceeded it by ten or twenty pounds, in all probability his master will measure the next day's task accordingly.

———

Solomon Northup. *Twelve Years a Slave*. London: Sampson Low, 1853. Solomon Northup was a Northern free black who was drugged and sold into slavery in the South. It took twelve years to prove his case and be freed.

### Owner Viewpoint

The negro slaves of the South are the happiest, and, in some sense, the freest people in the world. The children and the aged and infirm work not at all, and yet have all the comforts and necessaries of life provided for them. They enjoy liberty, because they are oppressed neither by care nor labor. The women do little hard work, and are protected from the despotism of their husbands by their masters. The negro men and stout boys work, on the average, in good weather, not more than nine hours a day. The balance of their time is spent in perfect abandon. Besides, they have their Sabbaths and holidays. White men, with so much of license and liberty, would die of ennui; but negroes luxuriate in corporeal and mental repose. With their faces upturned to the sun, they can sleep at any hour; and quiet sleep is the greatest of human enjoyments. "Blessed be the man who invented sleep." 'Tis happiness in itself—and results from contentment with the present, and confident assurance of the future.

———

George Fitzhugh. *Cannibals All! or Slaves Without Masters*. Richmond, Va.: A. Morris, 1857. George Fitzhugh wrote proslavery articles for the *Richmond Examiner*, a widely read Southern newspaper.

### Abolitionist Viewpoint

While we bestow our earnest disapprobation on the system of slavery, let us not flatter ourselves that we are in reality any better than our brethren of the South. Thanks to our soil and climate, and the early exertions of the Quakers, the *form* of slavery does not exist among us; but the very *spirit* of the hateful and mischievous thing is here in all its strength. The manner in which we use what power we have, gives us ample reason to be grateful that the nature of our institutions does not intrust us with more. Our prejudice against colored people is even more inveterate than it is at the South. The planter is often attached to the negroes, and lavishes caresses and kind words upon them, as he would on a favorite hound: but our cold-hearted, ignoble prejudice admits of no exception—no intermission. . . .

Those who are kind and liberal on all other subjects, unite with the selfish and the proud in their unrelenting efforts to keep the colored population in the lowest state of degradation; and the influence they unconsciously exert over children early infuses into their innocent minds the same strong feelings of contempt.

———

Lydia Maria Child. *An Appeal in Favor of That Class of Americans Called Africans*. Boston: Allen and Ticknor, 1833.

## Party Lines

**Put the information below the chart under the party name to which it belongs. Some boxes will be blank.**

- General Winfield Scott
- Lewis Cass
- began as an antislavery party
- Ripon, Wisconsin
- James Buchanan
- secret societies
- divided into Northern and Southern factions

- Abraham Lincoln
- candidate Martin Van Buren
- John Brown
- Millard Fillmore
- Free Soil, Free Speech, Free Labor, Free Men, Frémont and Victory
- Stephen Douglas

- Free Soil, Free Speech, Free Labor, Free Men
- Zachary Taylor
- capitalized on the fear of immigrants and the Kansas-Nebraska Act
- Franklin Pierce
- avoided adopting a party platform

| Whigs | Republicans | Democrats | Free-Soilers | Know-Nothings |
|---|---|---|---|---|
|  |  |  |  |  |
|  |  |  |  |  |
|  |  |  |  |  |
|  |  |  |  |  |

## Fanning the Fire

**Winds of anger fanned the fires of discontent surrounding the slavery issue. The result of the flames is the mystery phrase. Put the answers to the following clues in the spaces below.**

1. In this doctrine, Stephen Douglas said that a territory could prohibit slavery.
2. This fanatical antislavery proponent staged a massacre and attempted a revolt.
3. This decision declared the Missouri Compromise unconstitutional.
4. These Southern extremists wanted the South to secede to keep the Southern way of life.
5. Because of the fighting there, Kansas territory became known as this.
6. This president ran without a platform and stressed his military merits.
7. Before landing in this harbor, some captains put their crews in chains.
8. This territory's population gained 80,000 in one year.
9. This Illinois senator proposed dividing the unorganized territory in two.
10. This man found gold on his property.
11. This man made a famous speech called the "Seventh of March" speech.
12. This Southern spokesman offered resolutions that said no one could prohibit a territory from having slaves until it became a state.
13. This was the nickname given to the men who had gold rush fever.
14. They wanted to leave slavery where it was but opposed its extension into new territory.
15. This compromise made California a free state, but offered an enforced fugitive slave act.
16. This senator proposed amendments in a last effort to save the Union.
17. This was a name for the mass migration to California of men seeking wealth.
18. This act suggested the repeal of the Missouri Compromise and called for popular sovereignty in the unorganized territory.

## Crossword Puzzle

### ACROSS

1. The South threatened this if Lincoln won in 1860.
5. Douglas's "Doctrine"
7. slave who was refused freedom by the Supreme Court
11. He was "honest."
12. Democratic victor in 1856
15. escape route for fugitive slaves
17. non-Republican, pro-Union party of 1860
18. site of tensions between proslavery border ruffians and antislavery free-staters
19. madman of Pottawatomie and Harpers Ferry
22. Their party split and died in the 1850s.
24. president of the Confederate States of America
25. Swiss rancher who lost his land to gold rush fever
27. destination of a rush of people in 1849
28. members of a certain antislavery political group
29. S.C. representative who broke his cane

### DOWN

1. fort of first fire
2. proposed a last-minute, unsuccessful compromise
3. Constitutional Union candidate of 1860
4. senator bloodied by Brooks
6. site of Kansas massacre of proslavery settlers
7. party offering two candidates in 1860
8. famous conductor on the Underground Railroad
9. won a narrow victory in the 1848 election
10. Douglas's act introduced to promote railroad interests
13. sovereignty that let residents decide slavery issue
14. debated Douglas in 1858 and defeated him in 1860
15. influential abolitionist novel
16. state of great 1858 debates
20. His proviso failed to limit slavery in Mexican Cession.
21. Brown attempted to incite a slave revolt at this ferry
23. wrote a successful piece of abolitionist literature
26. chief justice during Dred Scott decision

## Flag Day!

**Many of the troops who served in the Civil War carried high the flag of the state they represented. Use an encyclopedia to research your state flag.**

1.  Draw and color the blank flag below to make it look like your state flag.

2.  What do the colors on your flag signify? ____________________________________
    ____________________________________________________________________

3.  What are the objects present on your state flag? ____________________________
    What do they mean? ________________________________________________
    ____________________________________________________________________

4.  In what year was your state flag adopted in its present form? ________________
    ____________________________________________________________________

5.  Does your flag have a motto on it? ________ If so, what does the motto mean? ________
    ____________________________________________________________________
    ____________________________________________________________________

6.  If there are any animals on your flag, what do they represent? ________________
    ____________________________________________________________________

7.  If your state was involved in the Civil War, which side was it on? ________________
    ____________________________________________________________________

8.  Does your flag's design reveal which side it was on in the Civil War? ________________
    How? ________________________________________________________________

Name _______________________

## Who Am I?

**The following selection is a brief autobiography written in 1859. Read it and then answer the questions based on your reading.**

I was born February 12, 1809, in Hardin County, Kentucky. My parents were both born in Virginia, of undistinguished families. My mother, who died in my tenth year, was of a family of the name Hanks. My paternal grandfather emigrated from Rockingham County, Virginia, to Kentucky about 1781 or 1782, where, a year or two later, he was killed by the Indians, not in battle, but by stealth when he was laboring to open a farm in the forest.

My father at the death of his father was but six years of age. By the early death of his father, and the very narrow circumstances of his mother, he was, even in childhood, a wandering laboring boy, and grew up literally without education. He never did more in the way of writing than bunglingly to write his own name. He removed from Kentucky to what is now Spencer County, Indiana, in my eighth year. It was a wild region with many bears and other animals still in the woods.

There were some schools, so-called, but no qualification was ever required of a teacher beyond "readin', writin', and cipherin' to the rule of three." If a straggler supposed to understand Latin happened to sojourn in the neighborhood he was looked upon as a wizard. Of course, when I came of age I did not know much. Still, somehow, I could read, write, and cipher to the rule of three. But that was all. The little advance I now have upon this store of education I have picked up from time to time under the pressure of necessity.

I was raised to farm work till I was twenty-two. At twenty-one I came to Illinois—Macon County. Then I got to New Salem, where I remained a year as a sort of clerk in a store. Then came the Black Hawk war; and I was elected captain of a volunteer company, a success that gave me more pleasure than any I have had since. I went into the campaign—was elated—ran for the legislature the same year (1832), and was beaten—the only time I ever have been beaten by the people. The next, and three succeeding biennial elections, I was elected to the Legislature. I was not a candidate afterward. During the legislative period I had studied law and removed to Springfield to practice it. In 1846 I was elected to the lower house of Congress. Was not a candidate for reelection. From 1849 to 1854, in politics, and generally on the Whig electoral tickets, making active canvasses. I was losing interest in politics when the repeal of the Missouri Compromise aroused me again.

If any personal description of me is thought desirable, it may be said that I am in height six feet four inches, nearly; lean in flesh, weighing on an average one hundred and eighty pounds; dark complexion, with coarse black hair and gray eyes. No other marks or brands recollected.

1. How old was the author when he wrote this autobiography? _______________

2. How did his father's father die? _______________

3. What was the author's occupation most of his early life? _______________

4. How do you sense the author felt about the education system of his time? (Support your opinion with quotations from the excerpt.) _______________

   _______________

   _______________

5. From what success did he get his greatest pleasure? _______________

   _______________

6. How does it appear that the author got most of his education? _______________

7. What was his father's occupation as a young boy? _______________

8. Who is the author? _______________

## Change in Southern Lifestyle

**The following excerpt is from Mary Boykin Chesnut's *Diary from Dixie*. Read the entries and then answer the questions based on Mrs. Chesnut's perceptions.**

RICHMOND, Va., Nov. 28, 1863.—I gave a party; Mrs. Davis very witty; Preston girls very handsome; Isabella's fun fast and furious. No party could have gone off more successfully, but my husband decides we are to have no more festivities. This is not the time, or the place, for such gaieties. . . . Mr. Venable, of Lee's staff, was at our party, so out of spirits. He knows everything that is going on. His depression bodes us no good. To-day, General Hampton sent James Chesnut a fine saddle that he had captured from the Yankees in battle array. Charleston is bombarded night and day. It fairly makes me dizzy to think of that everlasting racket they are beating about people's ears down there. Bragg defeated, and separated from Longstreet.

Nov. 30.—Anxiety pervades. Lee is fighting Meade. Misery is everywhere. Bragg is falling back before Grant. Longstreet, the soldiers call him Peter the Slow, is settling down before Knoxville. My husband bought yesterday at the commissary's one barrel of flour, one bushel of potatoes, one peck of rice, five pounds of salt beef, and one peck of salt—all for sixty dollars. In the street a barrel of flour sells for one hundred and fifteen dollars. Spent seventy-five dollars today for a little tea and sugar, and have five hundred left. My husband laid the law down last night. I felt it to be the last drop in my full cup. "No more feasting in this house," said he. "This is no time for junketing and merry making.". . . He is the master of the house; to hear is to obey.

December 19th.—A box has come from home for me. Taking advantage of this good fortune and full larder, have asked Mrs. Davis to dine with me. Wade Hampton sent me a basket of game. We had Mrs. Davis and Mr. and Mrs. Preston.

Christmas Day.—Yesterday dined with the Prestons. Wore one of my handsomest Paris dresses (from Paris before the war). Three magnificent Kentucky generals were present, with Senator Orr from South Carolina, and Mr. Miles. Others dropt in after dinner; some without arms, some without legs; von Borcke, who can not speak because of a wound in his throat. Isabella said: "We have all kinds now, but a blind one," Poor fellows, they laugh at wounds. "And they yet can show many a scar." We had for dinner oyster soup, besides roast mutton, ham, boned turkey, wild duck, partridge, plum pudding, sauterne, burgundy, sherry, and Madeira. There is life in the old land yet!

My husband says I am extravagant. "No, my friend, not that," said I. "I had fifteen hundred dollars and I have spent every cent of it in my housekeeping. Not one cent for myself, not one cent for dress, nor any personal want whatever." He calls me "hospitality run mad." To-day, for a pair of forlorn shoes I have paid $85. Mr. Petigru says you take your money to market in the marketbasket, and bring home what you buy in your pocketbook.

February 23d.—At the President's, where General Lee breakfasted, a man named Phelan told General Lee all he ought to do; planned a campaign for him. General Lee smiled blandly the while, tho he did permit himself a mild sneer at the wise civilians in congress who refrained from trying the battle-field in person, but from afar dictated the movements of armies.

February 26th, 1864.—We went to see Mrs. Breckenridge, who is here with her husband. Then we paid our respects to Mrs. Lee. Her room was like an industrial school; everybody so busy. Her daughters were all three plying their needles, with several other ladies. Mrs. Lee showed us a beautiful sword, recently sent to the General by some Marylanders, now in Paris. On the blade was engraved, "*Aide toi et Dieu t'aidera.*" When we came out some one said, "Did you see how the Lees spend their time? What a rebuke to the taffy Parties!"

March 12th.—Somebody counted fourteen generals in church to-day, and suggested that less piety and more drilling commands would suit the times better. There were Lee, Longstreet, Morgan, Hoke, Clingman, Whiting, Pegram, Elzey, and Bragg.

March 15th.—Old Mrs. Chesnut is dead. A saint is gone and James Chesnut is broken-hearted. He adored his mother. I gave $375 for my mourning, which consists of a black alpaca dress and a crape veil. With bonnet, gloves, and all it came to $500. Before the blockade such things as I have would not have been thought fit for a chambermaid. Everybody is in trouble. Mrs. Davis says paper money has depreciated so much in value that they can not live within their income; so they are going to dispense with their carriage and horses.

Yesterday, we went to the Capitol grounds to see our returned prisoners. We walked slowly up and down until Jeff Davis was called upon to speak. There I stood, almost touching the bayonets when he left me.

I looked straight into the prisoners' faces, poor fellows. They cheered with all their might, and I wept for sympathy, and enthusiasm. I was deeply moved. These men were so forlorn, so dried up, and shrunken, with such a strange look in some of their eyes; others so restless and wild-looking; others again placidly vacant, as if they had been dead to the world for years.

CAMDEN, S.C., September 19th.—My pink silk dress I have sold for $600, to be paid in installments, two hundred a month for three months. And I sell my eggs and butter from home for two hundred dollars a month. Does it not sound well—four hundred dollars a month regularly. But in what? In Confederate money. Hélas!

A thousand dollars have slipped through my fingers already this week. At the commissary's I spent five hundred to-day for candles, sugar, and a lamp, etc. Tallow candles are bad enough, but of them there seems to be an end, too. Now we are restricted to smoky, terrabine lamps—terrabine is a preparation of turpentine. When the chimney of the lamp cracks, as crack it will, we plaster up the place with paper, thick old letterpaper, preferring the highly glazed kind.

Sherman is thundering at Augusta's very doors. My General was on the wing, somber, and full of care.

We have lost nearly all of our men, and we have no money, and it looks as if we had taught the Yankees how to fight since Manassas. Our best and bravest are under the sod; we should have to wait till another generation grows up. Here we stand, despair in our hearts . . . with our houses burning, or about to be, over our heads. The North have just got things ship-shape; a splendid army, perfectly disciplined, with new levies coming in day and night. Their gentry do not go into the ranks. They hardly know there is war up there.

Serena's account of money spent: Paper and envelopes, $12.00; tickets to concert, $10.00; toothbrush, $10.00; total, $32.00. To-day Mrs. McCord exchanged $16,000 in Confederate bills for $300 in gold—sixteen thousand for three hundred.

CHESTER, S.C., April 7th.—Richmond has fallen and I have no heart to write about it. Grant broke through our lines and Sherman cut through them. Stoneman is this side of Danville. They are too many for us. Everything is lost in Richmond, even our archives. Blue-black is our horizon.

April 22, 1865.—It has been a wild three days, with aides galloping around with messages, Yankees hanging over us like a sword of Damocles. We have been in queer straits.

CAMDEN, S.C., May 2, 1865.—Since we left Chester nothing but solitude, nothing but tall, blackened chimneys, to show that any man has ever trod this road before. This is Sherman's track. It is hard not to curse him. I wept incessantly at first. The roses of the gardens are already hiding the rains. My husband said Nature is a wonderful renovator. He tried to say something else and then I shut my eyes and made a vow that if we were a crusht people, crusht by weight, I would never be a whimpering, pining slave. When we crossed the river coming home, the ferryman at Chesnut's Ferry asked for his fee. Among us all we could not muster the small silver coin he demanded. There was poverty for you.

## Use highlighters or colored pencils to mark the following passages.

- Underline in red the passages that show Mrs. Chesnut's extravagances in spending.

- Circle in blue the passages that reveal the low value of the Confederate currency.

- Highlight in yellow the passages that indicate how the war was actually proceeding.

- Put brackets around passages that display changes that Mrs. Chesnut made in her lifestyle.

- For extra credit:

  Give an approximate translation of the quotation on General Lee's sword. With the Bible as your reference point, evaluate the philosophy of the quotation.


What was "the sword of Damocles"? Why would Mrs. Chesnut have referred to it in relation to the Confederate situation on April 22, 1865?

## Battle Cry!

**Fill in the gaps in these major Civil War battle outlines.**

I.  First Battle of Manassas
    A. Other Name:
    B. Date:
    C. Commanders
        1. Union:
        2. Confederate:

    D. Winning Side:
    E. Strategy:

    F. Consequences:

II.  Battle of Shiloh
     A. Other Name:
     B. Date:
     C. Commanders
         1. Union:
         2. Confederate:
     D. Winning Side:
     E. Strategy:

     F. Consequences:

III.  Second Battle of Manassas
      A. Other Name:
      B. Date:
      C. Commanders
          1. Union:
          2. Confederate:

      D. Winning Side:
      E. Strategy:

      F. Consequences:

IV.  Battle of Antietam
     A. Other Name:
     B. Date:
     C. Commanders
         1. Union:
         2. Confederate:
     D. Winning Side:
     E. Strategy:

     F. Consequences:

V.  Battle of Gettysburg
    A  Date:
    B. Commanders
        1. Union:
        2. Confederate:

    C. Winning Side:
    D. Strategy:

    E. Consequences:

VI.  Battle of Atlanta
     A. Date:
     B. Commanders
         1. Union:
         2. Confederate:
     C. Winning Side:
     D. Strategy:

     E. Consequences:

## Terms of Surrender

**A series of letters were exchanged between General Lee and General Grant finalizing surrender terms at the end of the Civil War. Place yourself in the positions of each of these men and write a brief letter from each man. One letter should be from General Grant outlining the terms of surrender and the other from General Lee responding to those terms.**

General Grant to General Lee: _______________________

_______________________

_______________________

_______________________

_______________________

_______________________

_______________________

_______________________

_______________________

_______________________

_______________________

_______________________

_______________________

_______________________

_______________________

General Lee to General Grant:

_______________________

_______________________

_______________________

_______________________

_______________________

_______________________

_______________________

_______________________

_______________________

_______________________

_______________________

_______________________

_______________________

_______________________

## Reflections of Life

**Underline the word or phrase that makes the statement correct.**

1. Frenchman Louis Daguerre developed an imaging process called the *(daguerreotype, ferrotype)* which used *(enameled iron, silver-coated copper plate)* on which to capture the image.

2. *Carte-de-visite* or *(cabinet, visiting card)* photographs were small photographs that were popular to exchange with friends and family.

3. George *(Eastman, Kodak)* developed roll film, which helped make photography affordable.

4. The lifestyle of the western Indians was documented by *(Mathew Brady, Edward Curtis)* at the same time that William Henry Jackson was capturing the *(beauty of the West, atrocities of war)*.

5. *(Mathew Brady, Alexander Gardner)* photographed a dead soldier twice, moving the body so that he could call it a Union soldier and a Confederate soldier.

6. A form of home entertainment that featured three-dimensional views of faraway places was the *(triplograph, stereograph)*.

7. A turn-of-the-century camera whose improvements allowed amateurs easy loading and unloading of film was the *(Swinger, Brownie)*.

8. The first significant use of the camera in battle was during the *(Civil, Crimean)* War.

9. In the late 1830s, Louis Daguerre and *(Alfred Stieglitz, William Talbot)* developed photography independently.

10. *(Roll film, Faster shutter speed)* made it possible to market hand-held cameras.

Imagine that you are a person in one of the photographs in the chapter and write a first-person story about it.

_______________________________________________________________

_______________________________________________________________

_______________________________________________________________

_______________________________________________________________

_______________________________________________________________

_______________________________________________________________

_______________________________________________________________

_______________________________________________________________

_______________________________________________________________

_______________________________________________________________

## What Do You See?

**Look at the pictures on the following pages in the textbook. Give your impression of what you see in the photograph and the idea you think the photographer is trying to convey.**

1. Page 321— ________________________________________

   ________________________________________

   ________________________________________

   ________________________________________

   ________________________________________

   ________________________________________

2. Page 323— ________________________________________

   ________________________________________

   ________________________________________

   ________________________________________

   ________________________________________

   ________________________________________

3. Page 324— ________________________________________

   ________________________________________

   ________________________________________

   ________________________________________

   ________________________________________

   ________________________________________

4. Page 327— ________________________________________

   ________________________________________

   ________________________________________

   ________________________________________

   ________________________________________

5. Page 328— ________________________________________

   ________________________________________

   ________________________________________

   ________________________________________

   ________________________________________

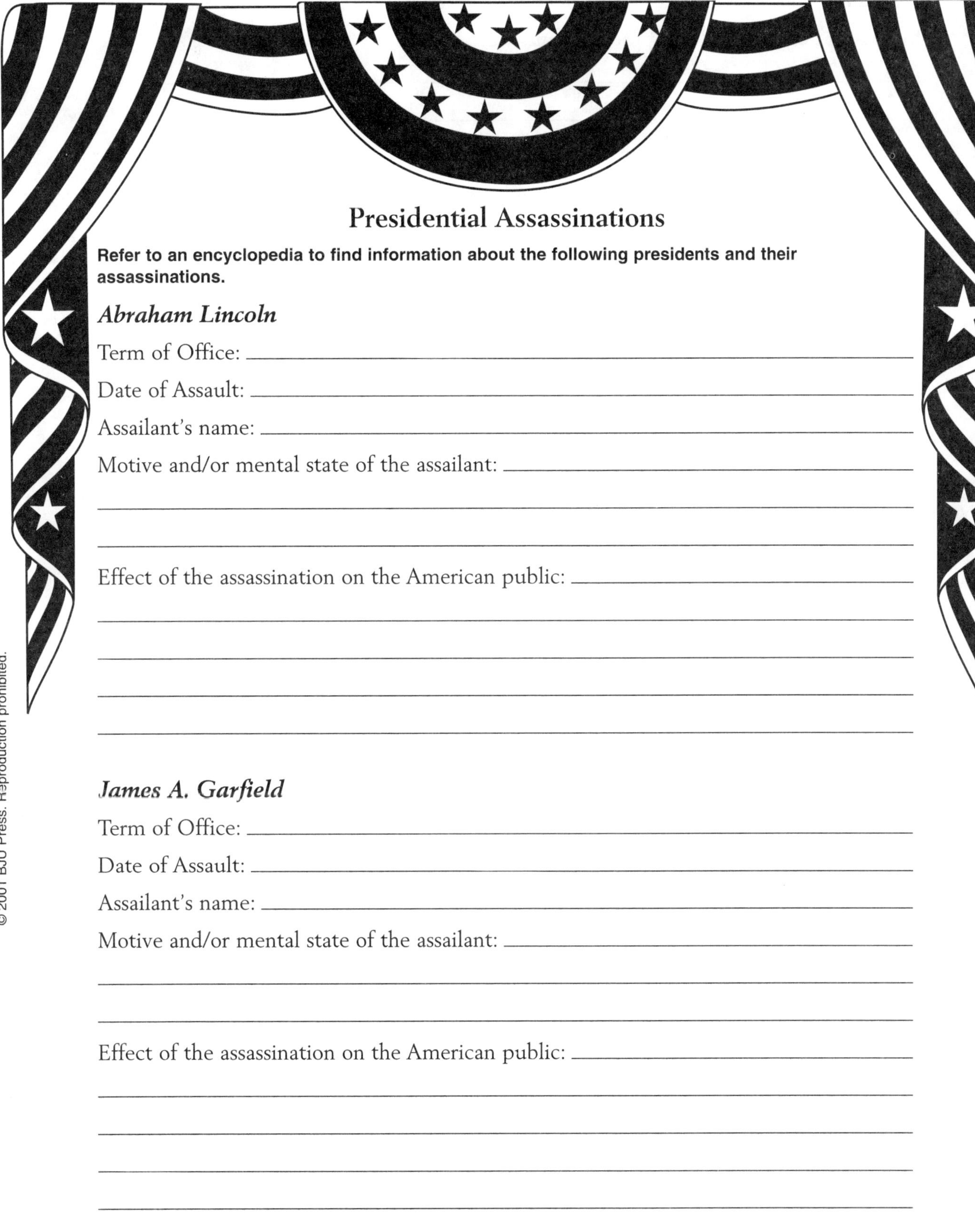

## Presidential Assassinations

**Refer to an encyclopedia to find information about the following presidents and their assassinations.**

### Abraham Lincoln

Term of Office: _______________________________________________________

Date of Assault: ______________________________________________________

Assailant's name: _____________________________________________________

Motive and/or mental state of the assailant: __________________________

_______________________________________________________________________

_______________________________________________________________________

Effect of the assassination on the American public: ___________________

_______________________________________________________________________

_______________________________________________________________________

_______________________________________________________________________

_______________________________________________________________________

_______________________________________________________________________

### James A. Garfield

Term of Office: _______________________________________________________

Date of Assault: ______________________________________________________

Assailant's name: _____________________________________________________

Motive and/or mental state of the assailant: __________________________

_______________________________________________________________________

_______________________________________________________________________

Effect of the assassination on the American public: ___________________

_______________________________________________________________________

_______________________________________________________________________

_______________________________________________________________________

_______________________________________________________________________

### *William McKinley*

Term of Office: _______________________________________________________

Date of Assault: _______________________________________________________

Assailant's name: _______________________________________________________

Motive and/or mental state of the assailant: _____________________________

_______________________________________________________________________

_______________________________________________________________________

Effect of the assassination on the American public: ______________________

_______________________________________________________________________

_______________________________________________________________________

_______________________________________________________________________

_______________________________________________________________________


### *John F. Kennedy*

Term of Office: _______________________________________________________

Date of Assault: _______________________________________________________

Assailant's name: _______________________________________________________

Motive and/or mental state of the assailant: _____________________________

_______________________________________________________________________

Effect of the assassination on the American public: ______________________

_______________________________________________________________________

_______________________________________________________________________

_______________________________________________________________________

_______________________________________________________________________

What precautions are now taken to protect the president? _________________

_______________________________________________________________________

_______________________________________________________________________

_______________________________________________________________________

_______________________________________________________________________

_______________________________________________________________________

## Checking Up on Reconstruction

**Show which Reconstruction plan each statement describes by placing a check in the correct box or boxes.**

**Lincoln's Plan**
  **Johnson's Plan**
    **Radical Republicans' Plan**

☐ ☐ ☐    1. viewed Southerners as rebellious members of the Union

☐ ☐ ☐    2. decided to appoint military governors

☐ ☐ ☐    3. demanded the abolition of slavery

☐ ☐ ☐    4. believed Reconstruction was up to the president

☐ ☐ ☐    5. denied suffrage and political office to former Confederate leaders

☐ ☐ ☐    6. wanted a "ten per cent" plan with stricter qualifications

☐ ☐ ☐    7. promoted the Wade-Davis Bill

☐ ☐ ☐    8. viewed the South as conquered enemies

☐ ☐ ☐    9. wanted to grant presidential pardons

☐ ☐ ☐    10. wanted majority of Southern males to take an oath of allegiance

### *Take It Further*

11. The Radicals made an attempt to limit the power of the president. One bill called the

    ______________ of ______________ Act was an attempt to retain ______________

    ______________ as secretary of war since he was an important Radical in the cabinet.

12. How did President Johnson react to this congressional act? ______________

    What did Congress do then? ______________

    ______________

13. How would Johnson's removal have affected future presidential power? ______________

    ______________

    ______________

14. Three amendments made during Reconstruction had consequences that reach into our

    twentieth-century legislation. The amendments were the ______________,

    ______________, and ______________.

15. Using the Appendix, pages 670-71, determine which amendment(s) the Black Codes

    tried to bypass and explain how they were able to do it. ______________

    ______________

    ______________

    ______________

## Jests and Jabs

**Analyze the following Nast political cartoon, taken from *The Art and Politics of Thomas Nast* by Morton Keller (Oxford University Press). Tell who the people are, whom the animals represent, and what you think Nast was trying to say.**

_______________________________

_______________________________

_______________________________

_______________________________

_______________________________

_______________________________

_______________________________

_______________________________

_______________________________

_______________________________

_______________________________

_______________________________

_______________________________

_______________________________

_______________________________

_______________________________

_______________________________

_______________________________

_______________________________

**In the box, draw a political cartoon about an issue, either state or national, that is currently in the news.**

## Exposé

**Grant's administrative era was filled with political scandal within and without. Summarize the following scandals using the terms given.**

### *The Tammany Hall Scandal*

Tammany Hall was a political organization originally started in the late 1700s to protect poorer citizens from the control of those with property. It later became an organization of the middle class which, when property qualifications for voting were lifted, began to take control of the New York City government. How did Tammany Hall's control affect New York? *(Terms: "Boss" Tweed, corruption, bribes, cartoons, reform)*

### *The Credit Mobilier Scandal*

This scandal occurred when Credit Mobilier managed to buy the outstanding stock of the Union Pacific Railroad and reissue it to Credit Mobilier stockholders so that both companies had the same owners. How did they make money this way and keep from being investigated? *(Terms: market value, Schuyler Colfax, 1872)*

### *The Gold Scandal*

This scandal occurred when two men tried to gain control of the gold supply. How did they plan to make a profit from this scheme, and why was their attempt unsuccessful? *(Terms: Fisk and Gould, federal treasury, Black Friday)*

### *The Whiskey Ring Scandal*

This scandal involved one of Grant's closest acquaintances. Who was this acquaintance, and how was this scandal carried out? *(Terms: excise taxes, character witness, tax collectors)*

## Presidential Insights

**The following are quotes from President Rutherford B. Hayes's *Diary and Letters.* What insights do the quotes give concerning the nineteenth president of the United States?**

1. **As a college student:** It is another intention of mine, that after I have commenced in life, whatever may be my ability or station, to preserve a reputation for honesty and benevolence; and if ever I am a public man I will never do anything inconsistent with the character of a true friend and good citizen. To become such a man I shall necessarily have to live in accordance with the precepts of the Bible, which I firmly believe, although I have never made them strictly the "rule of my conduct.". . .

   Insight—_________________________________________________________________

   _________________________________________________________________________

2. **On marriage:** The dear friend who is to share with me the joys and ills of our earthly being grows steadily nearer and dearer to me. A better wife I never hope to have. . . . Let me strive to be as true to her as she is to me. . . .

   Insight—_________________________________________________________________

   _________________________________________________________________________

3. **On the birth of his first child:** For the "lad" my feeling has yet to grow a great deal. I prize him and rejoiced to have him, and when I take him in my arms begin to feel a father's love and interest, hope and pride, enough to know what feeling will be if not what it is. . . .

   Insight—_________________________________________________________________

   _________________________________________________________________________

4. **On joining the army for the Civil War:** This was a just and necessary war and . . . it demanded the whole power of the country; . . . I would prefer to go into it if I knew I was to die or be killed in the course of it, than to live through and after it without taking any part in it. . . .

   Insight—_________________________________________________________________

   _________________________________________________________________________

5. **On politics:** Nothing brings out the lower traits of human nature like office-seeking. Men of good character and impulses are betrayed by it into all sorts of meanness.

   Insight—_________________________________________________________________

   _________________________________________________________________________

6. **On Christianity:** I am not a subscriber to any creed. . . . I try to be a Christian. . . . I want to be a Christian and to help do Christian work. . . .

   Insight—_________________________________________________________________

   _________________________________________________________________________

## Building a Monopoly

**A monopoly occurs when one person, business, or organization has complete control over a commercial activity. The following are six forms of monopolies. Put the letter of the monopoly next to the examples that match it.**

A. **horizontal integration:** One company totally controls one level of production.

B. **vertical integration:** One company controls all aspects of production from start to finish.

C. **trust:** Several companies join their stock into one trust which controls prices.

D. **pooling:** Two or more competing companies share profits, thus eliminating competition.

E. **holding company:** Two or more companies give 51 percent of their stock to a holding company. The major stockholders in the individual companies also hold stock in the holding company. Since the holding company is not producing anything and has no management expenses, when it sells its own stock, the money it makes is total profit to all the stockholders involved.

F. **interlocking directorates:** Two or more companies have the same board of directors, thereby reducing competition.

________ 1. The Crazy Cracker Company owns all the cracker-baking facilities in the U.S.

________ 2. Even though the Matthews Corporation doesn't produce anything under that name, it does sell stock and actually holds majority stock in three other companies.

________ 3. The Click Railway and Clack Lines have decided to join their stock into a corporation called Clickety Clack Tracks. Each company will retain its name but will now get the profits from both companies.

________ 4. My annual stock reports show that the board of directors in three of the companies is identical.

________ 5. The Laughing Gas Company owns 70 percent of the petroleum production process from exploration to refining to sales. They laugh all the way to the bank.

________ 6. Three car manufacturers joined under the name Conglomerate Motors to unify pricing and increase profits.

________ 7. Woof and Warp Weavers has the only factory in America that can weave argyle socks.

________ 8. Mr. Clark owns the Comer Bicycle Shop. He also owns the steel mill, bicycle factory, and tire company. No one else in town sells bikes.

________ 9. My town has two fast-food restaurants. After several price wars, they decided to work together. Now when one runs a special, the other gets part of the profit. Our hamburgers cost more these days.

________ 10. The Balius Trucking Company and Creason Transport both gave 51 percent of their stock to a company named BC Trucking. BC Trucking sells its own stock, and the profits go to stockholders from both companies.

________ 11. Turner Heating and Air Conditioning is the only installation and repair company in town. Mr. Turner charges whatever price he wants for his services.

________ 12. The Credit Mobilier company from the previous chapter changed its corporate structure to get more profits.

## Men Who Made a Difference

**Use an encyclopedia to find the contribution made by each of the following men, and then answer the questions.**

### George Eastman
What are the dates of his birth and death? _______________________

What was his other occupation? _______________________

Name his first invention and the year he invented it. _______________________

Name his second invention and the year he invented it. _______________________

How did it affect American life? _______________________

_______________________

_______________________

After his success, Eastman gave money to what type of institutions? _______________________

_______________________


### Charles Martin Hall
What are the dates of his birth and death? _______________________

What was the date of his contribution? _______________________

What was his contribution? _______________________

How did the invention affect American life? _______________________

_______________________

_______________________

What company became the first producer of aluminum? _______________________

_______________________

What special honor did Hall receive? _______________________

### Elisha Otis
What are the dates of his birth and death? _______________________

What was the year of his contribution? _______________________

What was his contribution? _______________________

_______________________

What later improvement did he make to his contribution? _______________________

_______________________

What were two other inventions attributed to him? _______________________

_______________________

How did his contribution affect American life? _______________________

_______________________

_______________________

## Charting America's Growth

**Using the following table, make a line graph of the growth patterns in the five major U.S. cities. Use colored pencils or markers to make your lines match the color indicated below the city name. (These numbers show population changes within city limits. Population declines may be due to migration to suburban areas.)**

|  | New York (blue) | Los Angeles (red) | Chicago (green) | Houston (black) | Philadelphia (yellow) |
|---|---|---|---|---|---|
| 1850 | 696,115 | 1,610 | 29,963 | 2,396 | 121,376 |
| 1900 | 3,437,202 | 102,479 | 1,698,575 | 44,633 | 1,293,697 |
| 1950 | 7,891,957 | 1,970,358 | 3,620,962 | 596,163 | 2,071,605 |
| 1960 | 7,781,984 | 2,479,015 | 3,550,404 | 938,219 | 2,002,512 |
| 1970 | 7,895,563 | 2,811,801 | 3,369,357 | 1,233,535 | 1,949,996 |
| 1980 | 7,071,639 | 2,966,850 | 3,005,072 | 1,595,138 | 1,688,210 |
| 1990 | 7,428,162 | 3,485,557 | 2,783,726 | 1,654,348 | 1,585,577 |
| 2000 | 8,008,278 | 3,694,820 | 2,896,016 | 1,953,631 | 1,517,550 |

1. Extend each population line into the shaded area to predict the growth of each city to the year 2010 based on the information given.

2. Which two cities continued to grow during the recorded period? ___________________________
   ___________________________

3. What do you think caused the growth in those two cities? ___________________________
   ___________________________
   ___________________________

## The Gilded Age

**In each numbered line, underline the word(s) least related to the bold word.**

1. **realism**
   *Call of the Wild*        Twain            Homer            helpless man

2. **Jack London**
   Horatio Alger            naturalism       Darwinism        Stephen Crane

3. **Social Darwinism**
   survival of the fittest   competition      Rockefeller      cooperation

4. **croquet**
   baseball                 tennis           golf             bicycling

5. **profit**
   decorations              Jumbo            Woolworth        materialism

6. **Moody**
   urban evangelism         Sam Jones        gospel songs     Spencer

7. **Sankey**
   "Jesus Is Calling"       Moody            blind            gospel songs

8. **Carnegie**
   horizontal integration   philanthropy     steel            textile mill

9. **Rockefeller**
   horizontal integration   trust            Standard Oil     bobbin boy

10. **Vanderbilt**
    steamboats              Commodore        railroads        steel

11. **Morgan**
    philanthropy            stocks           300-ft. yacht    mergers

12. **Duke**
    marketing strategy      tobacco          steel            hydroelectricity

13. **Heinz**
    Pure Food & Drug Act    honesty          Christianity     financier

14. **mass production**
    standardized sizing     sewing machine   tailors          democratization

15. **communication revolution**
    business growth         typewriter       shorthand        telegraph

16. **Stalwarts**
    favored reform          hard money       high tariffs     spoils system

17. **Cleveland**
    Mugwumps                Conkling         mudslinging      Blaine

18. **Farmer's Alliance**
    Oliver Kelly            strikes          Grange railroad  regulation

19. **William Jennings Bryan**
    "goldbugs"              "Great Commoner" Christian        Populist party

20. **free silver**
    People's party          farmers          inflation        gold

## Map Study: Routes and Riches

**Refer to the map on pages x-xi of the text and a United States atlas to complete the map on the next page. Label all states west of the Mississippi River with their postal abbreviations found in the Appendix on page 658.**

1. Using the directions below, show the approximate route of the major railroads given. Label the railroad lines and the cities mentioned.
   - Great Northern—Fargo, North Dakota; north to Grand Forks, North Dakota; west along the northern borders of North Dakota and Montana; south to Spokane, Washington; west ending in Seattle, Washington
   - Northern Pacific—Duluth, Minnesota; to Fargo, North Dakota; west to the southern border of Montana; following the border northwest to Butte, Montana; crossing Idaho at the 48th parallel; through Spokane, Washington; then dipping southwest before ending in Tacoma, Washington
   - Union & Central Pacifics—Omaha, Nebraska; west along the Platte River to Cheyenne, Wyoming; to the east side of the Great Salt Lake; around the northern end of the Great Salt Lake; southwest to Sacramento, California; ending in San Francisco, California. Mark the map with an "X" at Promontory Point where the two lines joined.
   - Southern Pacific—New Orleans, Louisiana; west to San Antonio, Texas; to the Rio Grande; northwest to El Paso, Texas; west to Tucson, Arizona; northwest to the Gila River; west to Yuma, Arizona; northwest ending in Los Angeles, California

2. Draw the approximate routes of the following cattle trails. Use colored pencils according to the color given next to each trail name. Label the routes and cities mentioned.
   - Goodnight-Loving Trail (blue)—Central Texas near the Colorado River; west to Pecos, Texas; north through New Mexico to Denver, Colorado; ending in Cheyenne, Wyoming
   - Western Trail (red)—north of San Antonio, Texas; north to the Texas border; northwest to Dodge City, Kansas; northwest ending in Ogallala, Nebraska
   - Chisholm Trail (green)—south of San Antonio, Texas (east of the Western Trail); north to Abilene, Kansas
   - Sedalia Trail (yellow)—south of San Antonio, Texas (east of Chisholm Trail); north to Fort Worth, Texas; northeast to Sedalia, Missouri

3. Identify the following mining areas with their names. Next to the name, draw a yellow nugget if gold was mined, a gray nugget if silver was mined, and an orange nugget if copper was mined.
   - Pikes Peak, Colorado
   - Leadville, Colorado
   - Comstock Lode (south of Virginia City, Nevada)
   - Anaconda, Montana

4. Identify the early major meat-packing plant locations with the city name and a small cow.
   - Chicago, Illinois
   - Milwaukee, Wisconsin
   - Cincinnati, Ohio
   - Minneapolis, Minnesota

## Farming Fluctuations

**Use the following information to build three bar graphs showing the fluctuation in farming. Use markers or colored pencils. Use green for farmers, red for farms, and brown for acres. Optional Activity: Answer the questions on the next page using the graphs.**

| Year | Total Farmers (x 1,000) | Total Farms (x 1,000) | Total Acres (x 1,000) |
|---|---|---|---|
| 1880 | 21,973 | 4,009 | 536,082 |
| 1890 | 24,771 | 4,565 | 623,219 |
| 1900 | 29,875 | 5,740 | 841,202 |
| 1910 | 32,077 | 6,366 | 881,431 |
| 1920 | 31,974 | 6,564 | 958,677 |
| 1930 | 30,529 | 6,295 | 990,112 |
| 1940 | 30,547 | 6,102 | 1,065,114 |
| 1950 | 23,048 | 5,388 | 1,161,420 |
| 1960 | 15,635 | 3,962 | 1,176,946 |
| 1970 | 9,712 | 2,954 | 1,102,769 |

### Total Farmers (x 1,000)

1880  1890  1900  1910  1920  1930  1940  1950  1960  1970

35000
30000
25000
20000
15000
10000
5000

### Total Farms (x 1,000)

1880  1890  1900  1910  1920  1930  1940  1950  1960  1970

7000
6000
5000
4000
3000
2000

### Total Acres (x 1,000)

1880  1890  1900  1910  1920  1930  1940  1950  1960  1970

1,200,000
1,100,000
1,000,000
900,000
800,000
700,000
600,000
500,000

## Agricultural Assimilation

**Use the previous activity and the book to answer the following questions. You may need to go to other sources or ask your parents or grandparents for input.**

1. What decade shows the greatest numerical increase in farms, farmers, and total acres? What are some possible reasons for that increase?

   _______________________________________________

   _______________________________________________

   _______________________________________________

2. Which decade had the most numerical stability in all areas? Why could this have occurred?

   _______________________________________________

   _______________________________________________

   _______________________________________________

3. What decade shows a sharp decline in farms and farmers? What event occurred prior to that time that may have begun the decline and yet allowed an increase in farmed acres? How do you think that event affected the decline and yet allowed the increase?

   _______________________________________________

   _______________________________________________

   _______________________________________________

   _______________________________________________

4. Based on the decades from 1950 to 1970, what can we assume happened to farmers and farms from 1970 to 1990?

   _______________________________________________

   _______________________________________________

5. How is it possible that from 1950 to 1970 there were fewer farmers and farms and yet the amount of acreage being farmed remained stable?

   _______________________________________________

   _______________________________________________

   _______________________________________________

6. Why are there so many farmers and farms in 1880 and 1890 in comparison to the acreage they farmed? What does this tell about the shift in occupations in the United States in the past one hundred years?

   _______________________________________________

   _______________________________________________

   _______________________________________________

## Cartoon Comments

**Political cartoons are used to put a big message into a little package. Answer the following questions about the cartoons on pages 395 and 401 in the text.**

**Page 395**

1. Which character represents the United States in this cartoon? _______________________

2. How does the cartoon make you feel about the position that the United States is taking in this issue? _______________________

3. What countries is Uncle Sam holding back? _______________________

4. What do their intentions seem to be? Are they friendly or aggressive? _______________________
_______________________

5. What country is represented by the man in the background tipping his hat? What does his action signify? Why isn't he standing closer? _______________________
_______________________

6. What is being offered by the U.S. Commercial Expansion? _______________________

7. How is the Chinese man portrayed? What does his attitude seem to be? _______________________
_______________________
_______________________

8. Write a one- or two-sentence statement on how you think this cartoon would have influenced your opinions of the Open Door Policy. _______________________
_______________________

**Page 401**

9. What are the countries on the menu from which Uncle Sam may choose? _______________________
_______________________

10. Look in an outside source to find the present name of the Sandwich Islands. _______________________

11. Who is waiting to take Uncle Sam's order? _______________________

12. Use one word to describe how Uncle Sam appears to feel about the choices on the menu? _______________________

13. Write a one- or two-sentence description of how the United States acquired each of the countries listed on the bill of fare. _______________________
_______________________
_______________________
_______________________

14. Write a one- or two-sentence statement on how you think this cartoon would have influenced your opinions of United States imperialism. _______________________
_______________________

## Time Tells All

**Put the correct letter from the time line next to the term. Letters may be used more than once. In the other blank, give a short explanation of the term.**

________ 1. annexation of Hawaii ________________________

________ 2. *A Century of Dishonor* ________________________

________ 3. Custer's Last Stand ________________________

________ 4. the *Maine* sunk ________________________

________ 5. Alaska purchase ________________________

________ 6. Treaty of Kanagawa ________________________

________ 7. Wounded Knee Massacre ________________________

________ 8. founding of CMA ________________________

________ 9. Battle of Manila Bay ________________________

________ 10. Boxer Rebellion ________________________

________ 11. First Pan-American Congress ________________________

________ 12. Battle of the Washita River ________________________

________ 13. Treaty of Washington ________________________

________ 14. Dawes Act ________________________

________ 15. founding of CAM ________________________

________ 16. Spanish-American War ________________________

________ 17. surrender of Chief Joseph ________________________

________ 18. Open Door Policy proposed ________________________

________ 19. annexation of Midway ________________________

________ 20. Indian citizenship ________________________

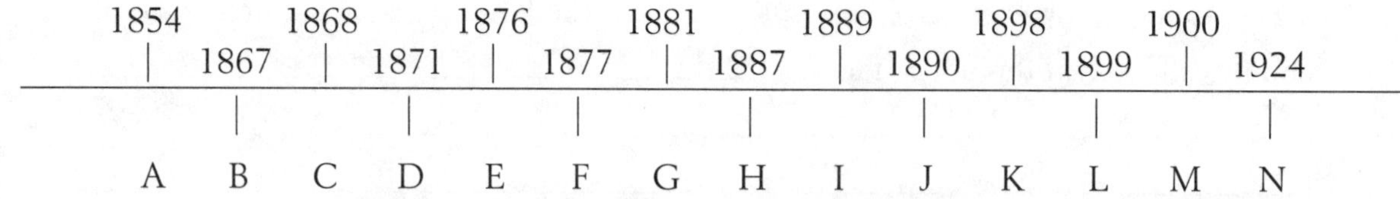

## Into the Sunset

**Complete the following narrative passage.**

Many of the stories told about the cowboys of the Wild West are more rumor than reality. Wild West heroes such as James Butler Hickok, better known as (1) "___________ ___________" were actually cold-blooded killers. Law and order were needed on the frontier, but because the cowboys lived on the edge of Indian territory, the law often did not reach them. When it did, it took many forms. The low man on the law enforcement ladder was the (2) ___________. Next came the county sheriff, who was able to appoint (3) ___________ to serve under him. Finally there were U.S. marshals and judges, who were directly commissioned by the president. The most famous of these judges was (4) ___________, also known as the (5) "___________ Judge." Many times there were still not enough lawmen to protect so large a territory. The (6) ___________ shipping company suffered over (7) ___________ stage-coach robberies in one month. They hired the famous (8) ___________ National Detective Agency, which developed the first (9) "___________" file. We often think of the stage-coach bandit with a bandana over the bottom half of his face, but the cowboy most often wore the bandana, or (10) ___________, to keep the dust out of his nose and mouth when he trailed the herd. From head to toe, the cowboy was dressed for the job of herding cattle. His "Stetson" kept the sun and the rain off his head, and, though it did hold water, it couldn't really hold a full (11) ___________. His boots were narrow at the top to keep (12) ___________ out and pointed in the toe so he could slip in and out of his (13) ___________ easily. Although he had planned to make tents with it, (14) ___________ found that the *serge de Nimes*, or (15) ___________, that he had purchased could endure the tough wear of the cowboy. Blue jeans became the staple of the working cowboy. But not all cowboys rode the range. Bill Cody, better known as (16) ___________, found that people would pay to see the romantic image of the West. Thousands of people came to see the Indian chief (17) ___________ and the little woman (18) ___________, who could shoot a dime tossed in the air. People liked this romantic West so much that they wanted to read about it. In 1902, Owen Wistar wrote (19) ___________, a novel that set the western stereotypes for several decades. Two other authors, (20) ___________ and (21) ___________, took over where Wistar left off to become the best-known western novelists. Our perception of the Old West has also been shaped by the movie and television industry. The first western movie was (22) ___________. The 1930s' singing cowboy, (23) ___________, became an example of good behavior. This was quite a switch from the reality of the Old West.

## "Who Should Go West?"

**After the deaths of his wife and mother, Theodore Roosevelt moved to the Dakota Badlands to become a rancher. The following is an excerpt from Roosevelt's book "Who Should Go West." List the qualities Roosevelt thought those going West should possess and explain what you think Roosevelt means.**

To be able to follow the business at all, the man must be made of fairly stern stuff. He must be stout and hardy; he must be quick to learn, and have a fair share of dogged resolution; and must rapidly accustom himself to habits of complete self-reliance. If he wishes to lead a happy life, he must also be good-natured, for his companions will greet with the most merciless raillery the slightest timidity or clumsiness on the part of a beginner, and they are a class of men who will resent in the roughest and most effectual manner any exhibition of ill temper. Even after many months of patient practice it is rare that an Eastern-bred man attains to the perfection shown by the plainsman in the actual cow-boy work, such as throwing the rope, stopping a stampede, breaking a rough horse, etc. To make up for his shortcomings in these particulars, he must show especial excellence in other regards. He must work regularly, not by spasms; he must keep sober; must be always alert and ready, and willing to turn his hand to whatever comes up.

|  | *Roosevelt's Phrasing* | *Interpretation* |
|---|---|---|
| 1. | | |
| 2. | | |
| 3. | | |
| 4. | | |
| 5. | | |
| 6. | | |
| 7. | | |
| 8. | | |
| 9. | | |
| 10. | | |

## Progressive Terms

**Write the terms that complete the statements.**

1. The nomination of a party's candidate by popular vote is called _______________.

2. A petition to hold an election to remove an elected official from office is _______________.

3. A person or business that controls distribution and prices of a product or service is a

   _______________________________________________.

4. A man who serves as an administrator of city government is called a _______________.

5. People voting yes or no to accept or reject a law is a _______________.

6. Placing the power of government in the hands of the people is _______________.

7. City government that combines the duties of mayor and city council and gives them

   to a group of men is called _______________.

8. A form of government control designed to break up existing monopolies is called

   _______________________________________________.

9. A process in which voters introduce legislation by petitioning their legislators to

   consider some action is _______________.

10. Reform through direct government action is government _______________.

11. Breaking up monopolies and restoring competition to the marketplace is _______________

    _______________________________________________.

12. The voting method that reduced voter intimidation was the _______________.

13. One of the means of progressive reform was increasing _______________ efficiency.

14. The ideological movement favoring political and social reform through education, all

    class political participation, and direct government action was _______________.

15. Writers who exposed abuse and corruption were _______________.

16. Banning the manufacture, sale, and transportation of alcoholic beverages is _______________.

17. Progressives favored legislation that allowed _______________

    to organize and force businesses to negotiate fairly.

18. To _______________, progress was a process of the natural order that

    could be aided by government intervention.

19. Historian Tindall stated, "The cure for the ills of democracy was _______________."

20. Roosevelt was said to be in some ways the most "_______________" president since

    John Adams.

## Think About It!

**Give a short definition of each amendment listed and tell how it changed the previous system and what effects it has had since. Tell whether you agree or disagree with the amendment and be ready to defend your opinion. You may refer to the Appendix on page 671 and other sources.**

1. Sixteenth Amendment: ________________________________________

   ________________________________________________________________

   ________________________________________________________________

   ________________________________________________________________

   ________________________________________________________________

   ________________________________________________________________

   ________________________________________________________________

2. Seventeenth Amendment: ______________________________________

   ________________________________________________________________

   ________________________________________________________________

   ________________________________________________________________

   ________________________________________________________________

   ________________________________________________________________

   ________________________________________________________________

3. Eighteenth Amendment: ________________________________________

   ________________________________________________________________

   ________________________________________________________________

   ________________________________________________________________

   ________________________________________________________________

   ________________________________________________________________

   ________________________________________________________________

4. Nineteenth Amendment: ________________________________________

   ________________________________________________________________

   ________________________________________________________________

   ________________________________________________________________

   ________________________________________________________________

   ________________________________________________________________

## Cryptograms

**Use the clues to decode the words below. Then use the code to read the quotation at the bottom.**

1. Roosevelt's platform against Taft and Wilson

    Y G V   Y D N W C Y D B W H R

2. Roosevelt's foreign policy

    H I G D F   H C Z N B O   D Y Q   K D E E O   D   M W L   H N W K F.

3. Roosevelt refused to shoot a captured bear, and this was the result.

    N A G   N G Q Q O   M G D E

4. fair treatment and equal opportunity for men and women

    H J P D E G   Q G D B

5. The Northern Securities case gave Roosevelt this name.

    N E P H N - M P H N G E

6. the Progressive party nickname

    N A G   M P B B   R C C H G   I D E N O

7. Roosevelt's name for the writers who exposed abuse and corruption

    R P K F E D F G E H

8. Roosevelt's answer to the comment that his conservation policy would be a memorial to him

    M P B B O,   W ' Q   E D N A G E   A D S G   W N   N A D Y   D   A P Y -

    Q E G Q   H N C Y G   R C Y P R G Y N H.

9. Roosevelt did this in the election of 1912.

    N A E G V   A W H   A D N   W Y N C   N A G   E W Y L

Presidents are people too. Although he was head of the nation, Roosevelt had this to say about his eldest daughter when he was asked if he could control her better.

W   K D Y   Q C   C Y G   C Z   N V C   N A W Y L H,   W   K D Y   M G

I E G H W Q G Y N   C Z   N A G   P Y W N G Q   H N D N G H   C E   W

K D Y   K C Y N E C B   D B W K G.   W   K D Y Y C N   I C H H W M B O

Q C   M C N A

## Map Study: Roosevelt Corollary

**Refer to the map on pages xii-xiii of the text and a world atlas to complete the map below.**

1. Label these countries with abbreviations:
   Cuba (CU), Mexico (MX), Haiti (HA), Virgin Islands (VI), Dominican Republic (DR), Puerto Rico (PR), Belize (BE), Guatemala (GU), El Salvador (ES), Costa Rica (CR), Honduras (HO), Panama (PN), Colombia (CL), Venezuela (VE), Nicaragua (NI).

2. Using a green pencil, color the country that controlled Panama prior to its independence.

3. Using a red pencil, color the country that was an alternate location for an Atlantic-Pacific canal.

4. Using a blue pencil, draw in the Panama Canal and label it.

5. Using a yellow pencil, color the country that became a commonwealth of the United States in 1898.

6. Using a purple pencil, color the two countries that were occupied by a U.S. Marine police force during Woodrow Wilson's presidency. (See page 448 of the text.)

## Presidential Programs

**In the blank provided, write the program or term described. Then put that answer in the chart under the correct president.**

1. put nearly one hundred million acres under federal control _______________

2. reform which lowered tariff and resulted in the first income tax _______________

3. American investments used to influence foreign affairs _______________

4. compromise between Russia and Japan which ended their war _______________

5.  fair treatment and equal opportunity for all motto _______________

6. The "Great White Fleet" was an example of this. _______________

7. He should have been hand-picked for this court position rather than the presidency.

   _______________

8. This made the United States a policeman over Latin America. _______________

9. He clashed with the president over public land use. _______________

10. Under this motto, there would be strong regulation, not trust-busting.

    _______________

11. This act balanced private banking and state-controlled banking. _______________

12. a five-man board to define and halt unfair labor practices _______________

13. built as a link between Atlantic and Pacific shipping _______________

14. labor's "Magna Carta" _______________

15. dealt with Pacific territorial claims and the Open Door policy

    _______________

| ROOSEVELT | TAFT | WILSON |
|---|---|---|
|  |  |  |
|  |  |  |
|  |  |  |
|  |  |  |
|  |  |  |
|  |  |  |
|  |  |  |

## Fundamentalists vs. Progressives

**Chart the conflicting views of fundamentalists and progressives on the following issues.**

| *Issue* | *Fundamentalists* | *Progressives* |
| --- | --- | --- |
| Government | | |
| Nature of Man | | |
| Improvement of Mankind | | |
| Problem Solving Methods | | |
| Leadership | | |

## Diary of a Soldier

**The following entries are from *Letters and Diary of Alan Seeger*, the diary of an eighteen-year-old American, Alan Seeger, who joined the French army within the first months of World War I—three years before American troops would be involved. Read the entries and then answer the questions.**

*Toulouse, Sunday, September 27, 1914.*—Fifth Sunday since enlistment. Beautiful sunny afternoon. Peace. The stir of the leaves; noise of poultry in the yards near by; distant church bells, warm southern sunlight flooding the wide cornfields and vineyards. Everything is ready for departure today.

*To his mother, Toulouse, September 28, 1914.*—We are still held up here, though all preparations for departure have been made and everyone expected to be off yesterday. We are entirely equipped down to our three days' ration and 120 rounds of cartridges. The suspense is exciting, for no one has any idea where we shall be sent.

*Sunday, October 11, 1914.*—This morning comes the unexpected news of the fall of Antwerp. This is the most important event of the war to date. It means the entire subjugation of Belgium. The Germans, as far as I can see, occupy all the territory they have coveted and all that they would keep in the event of their ultimate victory. It is my idea that they will now wage a defensive war entirely, limiting themselves to holding what they have. The impending winter will wonderfully favor them in this plan of campaign. The strong defensive lines they have reared on their front will enable them to detach large forces to cope with the Russians. On the whole, their situation seems good and the task of the French and English in driving them back a desperately hard one.

*To his mother, Aube, October 17, 1914.*—After two weeks here and less than two months from enlistment we are actually going at last to the firing line. . . . Imagine how thrilling it will be tomorrow and the following days, marching toward the front with the noise of battle growing continually louder before us. The whole regiment is going, four battalions, about 4,000 men. You have no idea how beautiful it is to see the troops undulating along the road in front of one.

*Vertus, October 20, 1914.*—Made a short morning's walk of 16 kilometers,—still through the great battle-field. The Germans retreated along the road we marched over. Extraordinary evidences of the artillery fire. Pine woods with the branches all ripped to pieces; large sized trees broken clean off in the middle. Today we passed through the villages of Marsain and Bergeres. The first was completely destroyed, not a house on the main street had escaped the fire. Nothing but blackened walls and here and there the inhabitants standing with sullen faces in their ruined doorways. The scene of the marching column down the ruined street,—a scene that will become familiar to us,—was imposing.

*November 10, 1914.*—Fifth day of our second period in the trenches. Five days and nights of pure misery. We came up here Thursday evening a foggy, moonlit night, bright enough to show the fields through which we ascended, spattered with shell-holes as thick as molehills, and the pine woods full of shattered trunks and broken branches. . . . Our position this time has been a claypit on a high summit above the chateau. Owing to its exposed and dangerous character very formidable bomb proofs have been built at this point of the line. To these we have been confined for five days from morning to night. A big hole here in the pit, a few yards from our door, marks the place where three men of Battaillon D were killed by a shell only a few days before our arrival. . . . It is a miserable life to be condemned to, shivering in these wretched holes, in the cold and the dirt and semidarkness. It is impossible to cross the open spaces in daylight, so that we can only get food by going to the kitchens before dawn and after sundown. The increasing cold will make this kind of existence almost insupportable, with its accompaniments of vermin and dysentery. Could we only attack or be attacked! I would hear the order with delight. The real courage of the soldier is not in facing the balls, but the fatigue and discomfort and misery. What a winter's prospect if our campaigning is only going to be alternate between these two phases of inaction and discomfort!

*On the Aisne, April 28, 1915.*—Patrouille! [Patrol!] How the heart beats to hear the word go round in the afternoon and to learn that one has been chosen to take part in it. To escape from the eternal confinement of the trenches, to stalk out into the perilous zone between the lines and there, where death may lurk in every thicket and uncertainty encompasses one close as the night, to court danger for several hours under a fine starlit sky, this is the one breath of true romance that we get in the monotonous routine of trench warfare. . . .

We went out, fifteen men, a few nights ago to reconnoitre a new ditch that had appeared on the face of the hillside high up under the German lines. . . . There were fruit trees all about this part of the hillside. They were clouded with bloom, reminding one of Japanese prints. But another odor as we advanced mingled with that of the blossoms, an odor that, congealed all through the winter, is becoming more and more intense and pervasive as the warm weather increases. Among the breaths of April, fragrant of love and the rebirth of life, it intrudes, the sickening antithesis—the odor of carrion and of death. . . .

Single or in heaps or files they lie—in attitudes of heroism or fear, of anguish or of pity—some shielding their heads with their sacks from the hail of shrapnel, many with the little "first aid" package of bandages in their hands, with which they have tried to stanch their wounds. Frenchmen and Germans alike, rigid bundles of soaked cloth, filling the thickets, sodden into the muddy beet fields, bare and exposed around the trenches on the bleak upper slope and amid sacks, broken guns and all the litter of the battle-field. The sight is one which may well be unnerving the first time, but one soon gets used to it, and comes to look upon these images of death with no more emotion than on the empty cartridge cases around them which, indeed, in a way they do resemble. Having served their purpose the material shell remains, while their vitality has been dispersed into the universe to enter into new combinations in that eternal conservation of energy which is the scientist's faith and that imperishability of anything that is beautiful in the human personality, which is the poet's.

*After spending another year and three months in entrenched warfare, Alan Seeger's dream would come true. He was in the first battalion to participate in the attack upon Belloy-en-Santerre on July 2, 1916. The following excerpt is from a reporter's account of the battle.*

The Legion attacks Belloy-en-Santerre. With a rush, it starts, its two leading companies pressing straight forward, beneath the crash of bursting shells, across a chaos of detonations. . . . Three hundred metres yet to cross and they will reach the enemy. . . . En avant! [Forward!]

But suddenly, hands relax their grasp, arms open, bodies stagger and fall, as the clatter of the German mitrailleuses [machine guns] spreads death over the plain where, but a moment before, men were passing.

*Epilogue*

*One of the first to fall was Alan Seeger. Mortally wounded, it was his fate to see his comrades pass him in their splendid charge and to forego the supreme moment of victory to which he had looked forward through so many months of bitterest hardship and trial. . . . So it was not until the next day that his body was found and buried, with scores of his comrades, on the battle-field of Belloy-en-Santerre.*

**Answer the following questions on a separate sheet of paper.**

1.  What was Alan's feeling about the war? Was he in the war for personal gain? How did he feel about trench warfare?

2.  Was Alan's opinion of the Germans' motive for war correct? What did the Germans actually desire? How did he view the French and English task?

3.  What evidences did the troops see of battle? How did the villagers appear to feel about the war and combatants?

4.  Why was patrol duty looked forward to? What did the men encounter? At the end of the April 28 entry, to what does "poet's" refer? What does this paragraph reveal about Alan's philosophy of life?

5.  Was Alan Seeger a hero?

## Poster Propaganda

**Analyze the four war posters on page 453 of the text. Answer the questions for each poster in the box relative to the poster's position on the page.**

1. How does the poster make you feel?
   _______________________________
   _______________________________
   _______________________________
   _______________________________

2. Why do you think the poster would make people want to buy bonds?
   _______________________________
   _______________________________
   _______________________________
   _______________________________

3. How has the artist aroused the desired emotions? ____________________
   _______________________________
   _______________________________
   _______________________________

1. How does the poster make you feel?
   _______________________________
   _______________________________
   _______________________________
   _______________________________

2. What is the message of the poster?
   _______________________________
   _______________________________
   _______________________________

3. How has the artist aroused the desired emotions? ____________________
   _______________________________
   _______________________________
   _______________________________

1. How does the poster make you feel?
   _______________________________
   _______________________________
   _______________________________

2. Why was the slogan "Remember Belgium" used? ____________________
   _______________________________
   _______________________________
   _______________________________

3. How has the artist aroused the desired emotions? ____________________
   _______________________________
   _______________________________
   _______________________________

1. How does the poster make you feel?
   _______________________________
   _______________________________
   _______________________________

2. Who is the woman supposed to be?
   _______________________________

3. What does the slogan "Every Garden a Munition Plant" mean? ____________
   _______________________________
   _______________________________
   _______________________________
   _______________________________

4. How does the artist convey the message? ____________________
   _______________________________
   _______________________________

## Map Study: The World at War

**Refer to the map on page 456 of the text and a historical world atlas to complete the map below.**

1. Label these countries with abbreviations: Germany (Ger.), Sweden (Swe.), France (Fr.), Denmark (Den.), Great Britain (G.B.), Belgium (Bel.), Netherlands (Neth.), Norway (Nor.), Spain (Sp.), Portugal (Por.), Italy (It.), Greece (Gr.), Bulgaria (Bul.), Serbia (Serb.), Austria-Hungary (Aus.-Hun.), Switzerland (Swi.), Russian Empire (Rus. Emp.), Ottoman Empire (Otto. Emp.).

2. Label the Argonne Forest, the Marne River, the Belleau Wood, and Château-Thierry.

3. Using a green pencil, color the Allied countries.

4. Using a red pencil, color the Central Power countries.

5. Using a blue pencil, color in the neutral nations.

6. Using a yellow pencil, draw in the line of the front in 1918.

7. Using a purple pencil, draw in the armistice line.

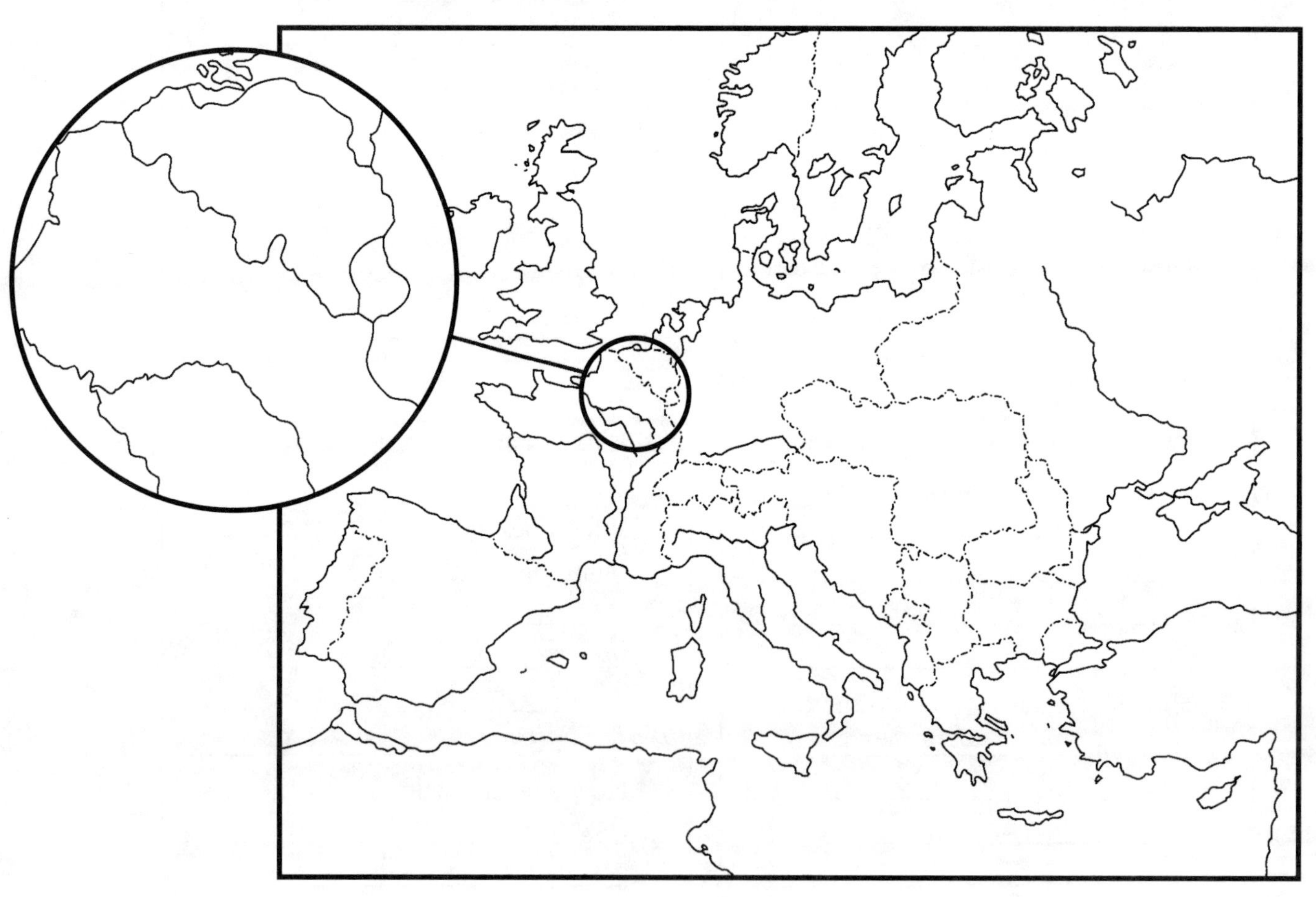

## Weapons of War

**Several new and improved forms of weaponry were used in World War I. Use an encyclopedia or other reference to fill in the following chart.**

| Weapon | Definition | Inventor | Battle Use | Effectiveness |
|---|---|---|---|---|
| Big Bertha | | | | |
| tank | | | | |
| airplane | | | | |
| submarine | | | | |
| chemical warfare | | | | |
| hand grenade | | | | |
| dirigibles | | | | |

## What's the Question?

**Here are the answers. Put the questions in the blanks provided.**

1. another way of talking about food saving and production _______________________

2. a general association of nations for the purpose of affording mutual guarantees of political independence and territorial integrity to great and small states alike

   _______________________

3. General John J. Pershing _______________________

4. German-Americans and Irish-Americans _______________________

5. They dominated the Versailles conference and were called the "Big Four." _______________________

   _______________________

6. April 6, 1917 _______________________

7. It was the ship that marked the violation of America's right to open sea travel.

   _______________________

8. the name given to President Wilson's statement that another attack on a passenger or merchant vessel would break ties with Germany and perhaps lead to war

   _______________________

9. It allowed a national draft to increase recruitment. _______________________

   _______________________

10. *"Es ist nichts, es ist nichts."* _______________________

11. Kaiser Wilhelm II _______________________

12. unofficial anthem of the American doughboy _______________________

13. It was the battle that turned the tide of the war. _______________________

14. Pancho Villa _______________________

15. It was a German policy which said that all ships in the war zone would be sunk.

    _______________________

16. It was the event that sparked World War I. _______________________

17. November 11, 1918 _______________________

18. Intercepted and decoded by the British, it called for Mexican support of the German cause.

    _______________________

19. He was America's "Ace of Aces." _______________________

20. Under these, it became a crime to criticize the war effort. _______________________

21. Wilson's plan for peace _______________________

22. January 28, 1919 _______________________

## Cartoon Capers

**Many a truth is said in jest. This was the way that J. Ding got the truth to the people in 1928 with the following cartoon. Look at the cartoon and answer the following questions.**

1. Who was Al Smith? ______________________
   ______________________
   ______________________

2. What does he say he wants to do for the farmer? ______________________

3. Does he look ready to help the farmer? ______________________

4. What does he look ready to do? ______________________

5. Who is his wife? ______________________

6. Does she look ready to work? ______________________

7. What does she have with her? ______________________

8. What do they reveal about her? ______________________

WANT ANY HELP ?

WESTERN FARMER

AL SMITH

DEM. PARTY

TAMMANY

FARM INTERESTS

9. Briefly tell what Tammany Hall was. (See Chapter 15 of the text.) ______________________
   ______________________
   ______________________

10. What is Ding implying by having Tammany in the picture? ______________________
    ______________________

11. What does the dog represent? ______________________

12. Do you think he can win against the tiger? (Explain) ______________________

13. Why does the farmer look perplexed? ______________________

14. In your own words, tell what you think this cartoon would have meant to people who saw it on June 4, 1928. ______________________
    ______________________
    ______________________

## Who's Who?

**Using the text, put the following terms in the chart under the correct president.**

| | | |
|---|---|---|
| hands-off approach | heart attack | "normalcy" |
| Teapot Dome scandal | engineer | Al Smith |
| into office by presidential death | World War I | Ohio Gang |
| secretary of commerce | depression | Albert B. Fall |
| governor of Massachusetts | Vermont | food relief |
| "The business of America is business." | newspaper editor | looked presidential |
| first Republican president of 1920s | Harry Daugherty | Charles G. Dawes |

| Warren G. Harding | Calvin Coolidge | Herbert Hoover |
|---|---|---|
| | | |
| | | |
| | | |
| | | |
| | | |
| | | |
| | | |
| | | |
| | | |

## Positive or Negative Influence?

**Write a brief description of each of the following 1920s personalities and describe their positive or negative influence on 1920s society.**

1. Charles A. Lindbergh, Jr.: ________________________

2. Al Capone: ________________________

3. William J. Bryan: ________________________

4. Albert Einstein: ________________________

## Scripture Search

**Read the following excerpt from the 1929 book *The American Omen* by Garet Garrett. Use the questions below to analyze the philosophy of finance evidenced in the book and manifested by many Americans before the stock market crash of 1929.**

People may ruin themselves by saving instead of spending. . . . It is now true for the first time in the economic annals of the race because the problem of production has been solved. How to produce enough, even more than enough, is no longer any problem at all. We continue to recommend thrift as a private and public virtue without realizing that when once you have solved the problem of production, then thrift universally and rigorously practiced—the kind of thrift that means doing with less in order to save more—is economically disastrous. . . .

We must mind that we spend enough—to keep our existing industrial machine going at ideal capacity, for unless we demand and consume what it is ready to provide, there will be unemployment, from unemployment underconsumption, and the rhythm of prosperity will break. . . .

Increasingly the anxiety of modern business is how to stimulate effective wanting, how to induce people in the average to exert themselves more in order to be able to have and consume more. Installment selling has that motive. Give a man on credit a better house in a better neighborhood, give him on credit a garage and a motor car to put in it, give him on credit all the goods that belong to a higher standard of living than he has hitherto thought himself able to afford, and what will he do? Will he give up these things because he cannot afford them? Not for that reason. Not for any reason whatever if he can help it. He will think of ways to increase his income. This means only that he will exert himself more to produce other things the equivalent of these, and that will be more than he ever produced before. From THE AMERICAN OMEN by Garet Garrett, copyright 1928 by E. P. Dutton, renewed. Used by permission of Dutton, a division of Penguin Putnam Inc.

1. In your own words, briefly summarize what the selection is saying. ___________________

   ___________________________________________________________________________

   ___________________________________________________________________________

2. Read Proverbs 6:6-11. Does this passage agree or disagree with the philosophy in this

   article? Explain your answer. ______________________________________________

   ___________________________________________________________________________

3. Now read Luke 12:16-34. Does this passage agree or disagree with the philosophy in

   this article? Explain your answer. ___________________________________________

   ___________________________________________________________________________

   ___________________________________________________________________________

4. Based on these two Scripture passages, what balance needs to be achieved in financial

   matters? __________________________________________________________________

   ___________________________________________________________________________

   ___________________________________________________________________________

5. Read Proverbs 22:7. How does this apply to installment buying? ___________________

   ___________________________________________________________________________

   ___________________________________________________________________________

## Make It Right!

**In the following paragraphs, several words or phrases have been numbered. As you read the page, decide if those numbered items are correct or incorrect. If they are incorrect, cross them out and write the correct word or phrase above them.**

After the war, the nation wanted to get back to business as usual, and [1] isolationism was the goal of all the people. Many things in the nation had changed with the needs of war. American farms had been feeding Americans and [2] Europeans. After the war, when the young men went back to the farm, they found that food prices had [3] plunged due to the [4] meager harvest of 1920. When they went to the city, they found war industries [5] closed. These factors combined to take unemployment to a high of [6] 18.3 percent.

The nation faced not only economic changes but also the emotional impact of war. Americans were warily looking for other enemies. They feared the [7] agnostics who had talked about overthrowing the United States government. This fear caused a temporary panic called the [8] Red Scare. It also helped reinforce the idea that it was time for America to take care of things at home. [9] Internal policy of the 1920s was [10] isolationism. However, America was now a world power, and with that power came responsibility for keeping the peace. The [11] Dawes Plan limited [12] air force capabilities by establishing a ratio of power among the five most powerful countries. Another interesting plan was the [13] Kellogg-Briand Pact, which declared war to be [14] inhumane. Closer to home, effort was made to improve relationships with [15] Canada.

With war behind them, Americans now had to get to the business of everyday life. Evolution, [16] Freudian psychology, and the [17] theory of actuality (time and space vary according to the location and motion of the observer) were causing people to question Scripture and longstanding moral values. The questioning even went into the mainline religions, resulting in major denominational splits. The fundamentalists left the Northern Baptist Convention and formed the [18] General Association of Rural Baptists. As the fundamentalists tried to hold the faith, one area their efforts centered on was the teaching of evolution in public schools. [19] John T. Scopes was the defense attorney in the Scopes trial and used [20] William Jennings Bryan as an expert witness for the Bible. The evolutionists lost the case, but the antievolutionists lost the publicity battle.

The 1920s were a time of material prosperity and spiritual depravity. What seemed like such a good time to many was about to come to an abrupt halt.

## Twenties Tangle

**Answer the questions. Unscramble the circled letters to form a phrase that describes the era in the chapter.**

1. The first commercial radio station came on the air with the call letters ___ ___ ___ ___ in ___ ___ ___ ___ ___ ___ ___ ___ (O) ___.

2. (O) ___ ___ ___ ___ ___ ___ ___ ___ ___ ___ ___ ___ ___ ___ ___ ___ was the heart-throb of many silent-movie fans of the early 1920s.

3. Suspicion of foreigners contributed to the passage of the ___ ___ ___ ___ ___ ___ ___ ___ ___ ___ ___ ___ ___ ___ ___ ___ (O).

4. The day the bottom fell out of the stock market is called ___ ___ ___ ___ ___ (O) ___ ___ ___ ___ ___ ___ ___.

5. The first "million-dollar gate" for sports involved boxer ___ ___ ___ ___ ___ ___ ___ ___ (O) ___ ___.

6. "The Lone Eagle" and "Lucky Lindy" were nicknames for ___ ___ ___ ___ ___ ___ ___ ___ ___ ___ ___ (O) ___ ___ ___.

7. The "Saint Valentine's Day Massacre" involved ___ ___ ___ ___ ___ ___ ___ (O) ___'s gang.

8. Fear of foreigners and blacks brought back the Reconstruction organization called the ___ ___ ___ ___ ___ ___ (O) ___.

9. The term ___ ___ ___ ___ ___ ___ (O) ___ ___ ___ is used to describe a stock market that is characterized by rising prices and optimism.

10. The "___ ___ ___ ___ (O) ___ ___ ___ ___ ___ ___ ___" of the 1920s caught the attention of the world with their disregard for moral standards and their rebellious behavior.

11. Henry Ford's original car design was replaced by the ___ (O) ___ ___ ___ ___ in 1927.

12. Shoppers of the 1920s found that they could buy now and pay later with an ___ ___ ___ ___ ___ ___ ___ ___ ___ ___ (O) ___ ___ ___ ___ ___.

13. Babe Ruth became known as the "___ ___ ___ ___ ___ ___ ___ ___ ___ (O) ___ ___."

14. Girls who flaunted their freedoms with short skirts, short hair, and boyish looks were called ___ ___ ___ ___ ___ (O) ___ ___.

15. Buying low and selling high is known as ___ ___ ___ ___ ___ ___ ___ ___ (O) ___ ___.

The

___ ___ ___ ___ ___ ___ ___    ___ ___ ___ ___ ___ ___ ___ ___

## Deep Depression

Only the very rich were able to weather the Great Depression with little discomfort. The average family found itself living from job to job and paycheck to paycheck, never knowing how long either would last. It is remarkable to look back and see how many things families did without and yet led a fairly normal existence. A partial list could include toothpaste (baking soda was substituted), cars, refrigerators or iceboxes, gas stoves, snacks, toilet paper (magazines or catalogs were used), toys, and other entertainment.

Everything that was used was taken care of or reused in a different function. Towels and sheets became washrags or dust cloths. Thin-soled shoes had cardboard or newspaper laid inside them. Seed sacks became towels or even dresses and curtains.

Industrious people looked for odd jobs to make ends meet between jobs or paychecks. Growing extra food in gardens, washing windows, doing yard or garden work, painting, and running errands all became moneymaking opportunities.

**Suppose a plunge in the stock market took place tomorrow and the United States was once again faced with a depression. In the spaces below, make a list (in order of importance) of items you could do without. Keep only the necessities!**

1. _______________________    9. _______________________

2. _______________________    10. ______________________

3. _______________________    11. ______________________

4. _______________________    12. ______________________

5. _______________________    13. ______________________

6. _______________________    14. ______________________

7. _______________________    15. ______________________

8. _______________________    16. ______________________

**Make a list of jobs that you could do to help your family make ends meet. Remember that these jobs must be things that people will need to have done even in times of depression.**

1. _______________________    4. _______________________

2. _______________________    5. _______________________

3. _______________________    6. _______________________

**Name three things that could be reused and ways that you would reuse them.**

Item                                      Reuse

1. _______________________    _______________________

2. _______________________    _______________________

3. _______________________    _______________________

## The ABCs of Economic Recovery

**Give the names of the following 1930s programs and organizations. Write a brief description of the purpose of each. Which president initiated each?**

1. POUR—________________________________________________

   ________________________________________________

2. PECE—________________________________________________

   ________________________________________________

3. NCC—________________________________________________

   ________________________________________________

4. RFC—________________________________________________

   ________________________________________________

5. CCC—________________________________________________

   ________________________________________________

6. AAA—________________________________________________

   ________________________________________________

7. NRA—________________________________________________

   ________________________________________________

8. TVA—________________________________________________

   ________________________________________________

9. PWA—________________________________________________

   ________________________________________________

10. WPA—________________________________________________

    ________________________________________________

11. FERA—________________________________________________

    ________________________________________________

12. CWA—________________________________________________

    ________________________________________________

13. FDIC—________________________________________________

    ________________________________________________

14. CIO—________________________________________________

    ________________________________________________

15. AFL—________________________________________________

    ________________________________________________

16. NIRA—________________________________________________

    ________________________________________________

## Dust Bowl Disaster

Many times in his effort to make a living with the least expense to himself, man has not taken the time to consider the long-term effects of his methods. At the beginning of the twentieth century, settlers poured into the Great Plains hoping to benefit from the fertile soil there. Unfortunately, they did not plan for the effect that their plowing would have on the region's ability to hold its topsoil.

In Genesis 1:26, God gave man dominion (control) over all the earth and told him to subdue it (bring it into bondage). In Genesis 2:15, He put man in the garden "to dress it and to keep it." The word for "keep" in that verse is also translated "watch" or "preserve." In this case, it implies having charge of. The earth is the Lord's, but He has put it into man's care. With this principle in mind, answer the following questions.

1. What events led to the "Dust Bowl" of the 1930s? _______________

_______________________________________________

_______________________________________________

_______________________________________________

2. What measures could have been taken to prevent the "Dust Bowl"? _______________

_______________________________________________

_______________________________________________

_______________________________________________

3. Give an example of a current ecological problem. _______________

_______________________________________________

4. What caused this problem? _______________

_______________________________________________

5. How could the problem have been prevented or its effect been reduced? _______________

_______________________________________________

6. In India, the main religion prevents people from eating "sacred cows," yet many people there go hungry. Do you think this action agrees with Scripture? Support your conclusion with Scripture. _______________

_______________________________________________

_______________________________________________

_______________________________________________

### Optional Discussion

Do you think the United States has a right to refuse to send Third World countries aid because they are cutting down the rain forests?

Name ________________________

## Forget Your Troubles

**In the midst of troubles, people look for diversions to take their minds off the current situation. Answer the following questions about popular depression-era diversions. Then fit the answers into the chart under the appropriate category.**

1. Futuristic scientific inventions, such as his "two-way wrist radio," made him popular with adults and children alike. ________________________

2. She started out as a child star and in adult life became an ambassador. ________________________

3. This infamous duo shocked the nation with their bloody spree of theft and murder. ________________________

4. Orson Welles's version of this story sent the unsuspecting nation into a panic over the invasion of aliens. ________________________

5. In an attempt to be the first woman to fly around the world, she disappeared in the Pacific. ________________________

6. The nation listened as this giant craft exploded. ________________________

7. This epic Civil War story, first introduced as a book, was dramatized at the end of the decade. ________________________

8. He introduced "swing" and was followed by a host of others. ________________________

9. This was the first feature-length cartoon. ________________________

10. Bruno Hauptmann was eventually convicted of this crime. ________________________

11. This little girl challenged the depression with courage and pluck. ________________________

12. Thousands of girls swooned to this man's crooning. ________________________

13. This man topped the most wanted list. ________________________

14. The serial adventures of this cowboy hero started with the William Tell Overture and "Hi-ho, Silver! Away!" ________________________

15. Dinosaurs and cave men appeared together in this Stone Age story. ________________________

| Real-life Drama | Comic Strips | The Big Screen | Radio |
|---|---|---|---|
|  |  |  |  |
|  |  |  |  |
|  |  |  |  |
|  |  |  |  |
|  |  |  |  |

## A Time of Tyrants

**Never before had the world seen tyrants in such cooperation, each with his own ultimate plan and goal but willing to use the others for a time to get closer to that goal. Use your book and an encyclopedia to answer the following questions about each leader.**

### Germany

1. Leader's name ______________________
2. What was he called? ______________________
3. What was his father's profession and economic status? ______________________
4. How did he come to power? ______________________
   ______________________
   ______________________
5. How long did he lead? ______________________
6. What was his party's name? ______________________
7. Give a brief summary of his effect on the German people. ______________________
   ______________________
   ______________________
   ______________________
8. What was his party's symbol? ______________________
9. When he was young, what career did this man want to pursue? ______________________

### Italy

1. Leader's name ______________________
2. What was he called? ______________________
3. What was his father's profession and economic status? ______________________
4. How did he come to power? ______________________
   ______________________
   ______________________
5. How long did he lead? ______________________
6. What was his party's name? ______________________
7. What was his first profession? ______________________
8. Give a brief summary of his effect on the Italian nation. ______________________
   ______________________
   ______________________
   ______________________
9. What was his party's symbol? ______________________

### *Soviet Union*

1. Leader's name. ___________________________________________

2. What did his name mean? ___________________________________

3. What was his father's profession and economic status? _________________

4. How did he come to power? _________________________________

   _________________________________________________________

   _________________________________________________________

5. How long did he lead? _____________________________________

6. What was his party's name? _________________________________

7. Give a brief summary of his effect on the Soviet nation. _______________

   _________________________________________________________

   _________________________________________________________

   _________________________________________________________

8. In an effort to increase his political power, this leader had millions executed in what
   are now called ________________________________________________.

9. What was his party's symbol? _______________________________

### *Optional Essay*
**Using the information above and an encyclopedia, answer the following essay questions.**

1. As you can see from the background information, all three of these leaders came from
   a working-class background. How do you think this affected their political decisions?
   How do you think it affected the nations' reception of them?

   _________________________________________________________

   _________________________________________________________

   _________________________________________________________

   _________________________________________________________

   _________________________________________________________

   _________________________________________________________

   _________________________________________________________

   _________________________________________________________

2. Of the three governments represented by these leaders, which two are most alike?
   Why are they different from the third? Explain.

   _________________________________________________________

   _________________________________________________________

   _________________________________________________________

   _________________________________________________________

   _________________________________________________________

   _________________________________________________________

   _________________________________________________________

   _________________________________________________________

## Map Study: The European Theater

**Refer to the map on page 516 of the text as well as an encyclopedia or a historical atlas to complete the map.**

1. Label the following:
   - Countries—Algeria (Alg.), Austria (Aus.), Belgium (Bel.), Czechoslovakia (Cz.), Denmark (Den.), Egypt (Eg.), France (Fr.), Germany (Ger.), Italy (It.), Libya (Lib.), Morocco (Mor.), Norway (Nor.), Poland (Pol.), Soviet Union (USSR), Tunisia (Tun.), United Kingdom (U.K.)
   - Cities—(Use the dots to locate.) Algiers, Berlin, Casablanca, Dunkirk, Leningrad, London, Moscow, Munich, Oran, Paris, Potsdam, Rome, Stalingrad, St. Lô, Tripoli, Warsaw
   - Regions—Rhineland, Sudetenland
   - Rivers—Rhine, Rhone

2. Color the following:
   - Yellow—Neutral nations in 1942
   - Red—Axis or Axis-controlled countries
   - Black line—the Maginot Line
   - Green—Allied or Allied-controlled countries

3. Locate and label:
   - ✹ —the Battle of Britain
   - ⸸ —Vidkun Quisling's treachery
   - ⚡ —first blitzkrieg
   - ⚑ —Operation Torch's three landing sites
   - **OH**—Operation Husky's objective
   - **D-day**—Operation Overlord site
   - → —General Patton's advance after D-day

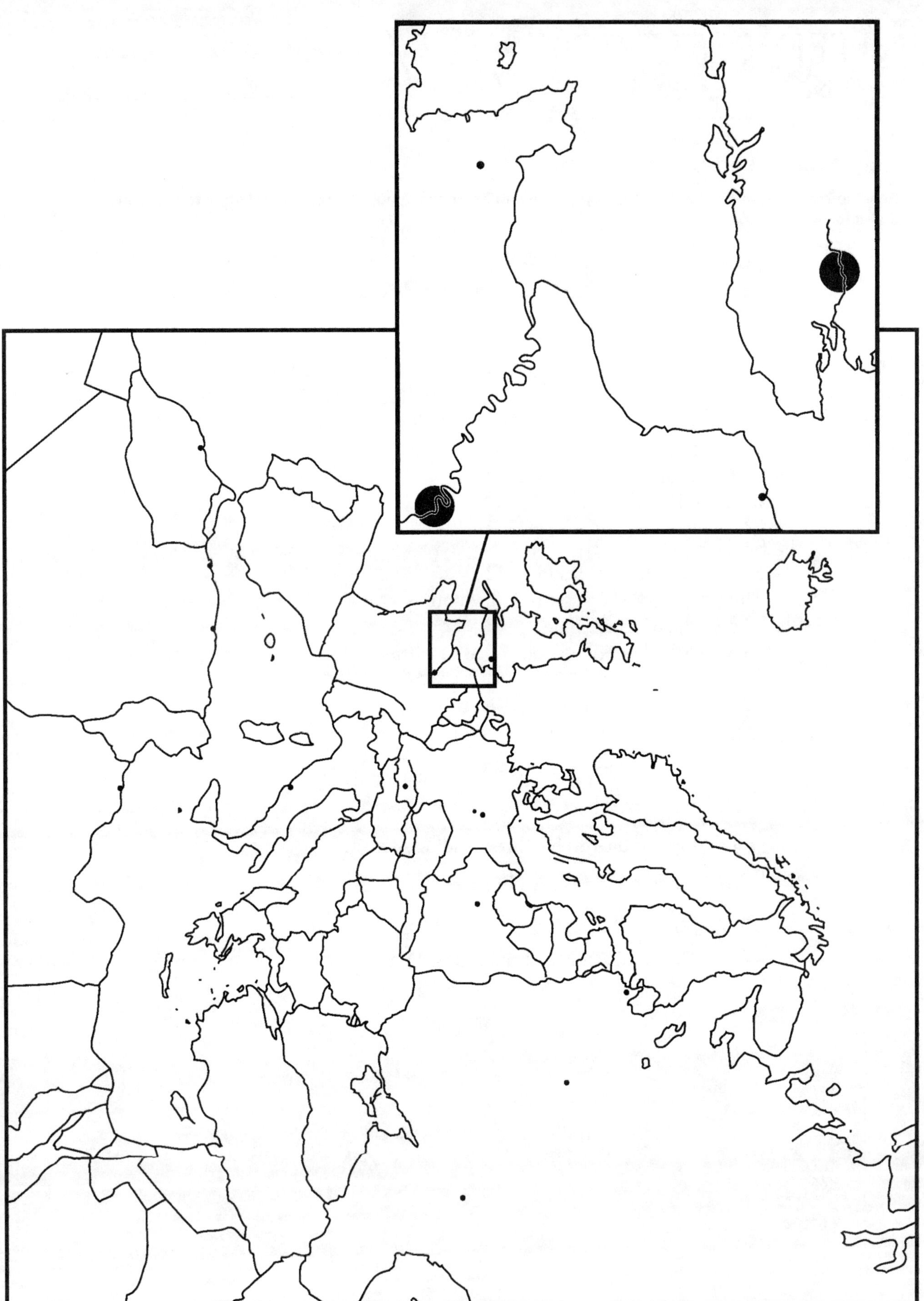

## Map Study: The Pacific Theater

**Refer to the map on page 528 of the text as well as an encyclopedia or a historical atlas to complete the map.**

1. Label the following:

   Countries—Australia, China, Dutch East Indies, French Indochina, Malaya, New Guinea

   Islands—Aleutian, Guadalcanal, Guam, Hawaii, the Marianas, Marshall, Midway, Solomon, the Philippines

   Places—Bataan Peninsula, Coral Sea, Manila, Tokyo

2. Draw a line showing the farthest extent of Japanese expansion in the Pacific.

3. Fill in the blank and label the map.

   a. What two Japanese cities were struck with a nuclear bomb? ______________________ and ______________________ Label each city on the map with a nuclear cloud.

   b. What location was bombed by the Japanese, bringing the United States into World War II? ______________________ Label the location with a bomb.

   c. What location was the site of the largest sea battle in history? ______________________ Label the location with a torpedo.

   d. What tiny island was the site of a battle where "uncommon valor was a common virtue"? ______________________ Label that island with a medal.

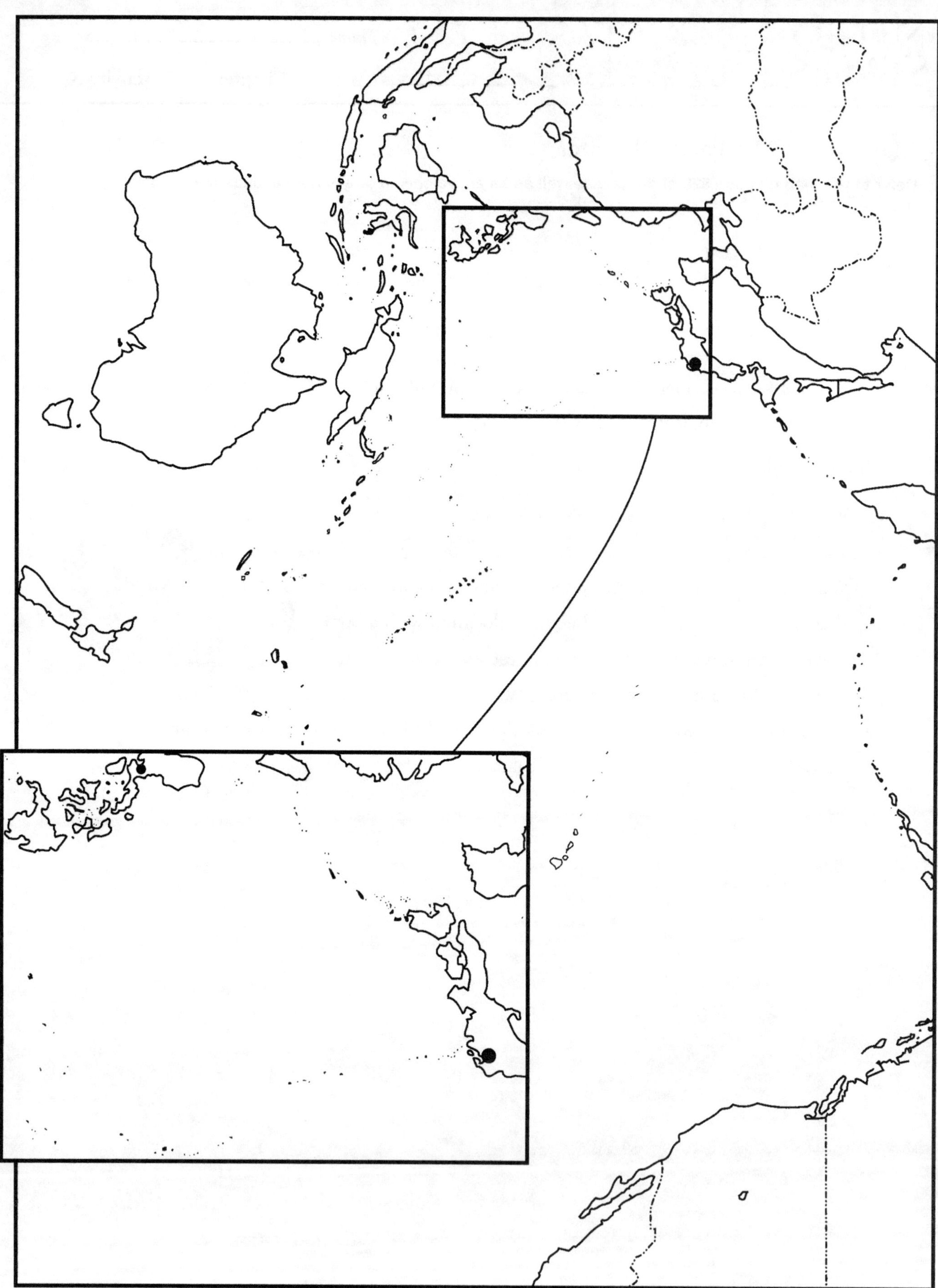

## Who, What, When, Where

**Answer the following questions.**

1. What was the German term for the "lightning war"? _______________

2. Who said "Your boys are not going to be sent into any foreign wars"? _______________

3. Where was the Atlantic Charter drawn? _______________
   _______________

4. When did the Japanese attack Pearl Harbor? _______________

5. Who said "I shall return"? _______________ To whom did he say it?
   _______________

6. Besides Okinawa, where did the U.S. want a foothold to Japan? _______________

7. What was the French Maginot Line? _______________
   _______________ What was its German counterpart? _______________

8. Who agreed to let Hitler take western Poland? _______________ What was
   their agreement called? _______________

9. Where did the Germans aim their attack in the operation code-named "Barbarossa"?
   _______________

10. What were three reasons that the United States stayed out of war so long?
    _______________

11. Who were the Nisei? _______________ What happened
    to them in America during World War II? _______________

12. Who symbolized the American women in industry during the war? _______________

13. What was a blue star banner? _______________
    _______________ What was a gold star banner? _______________
    _______________

14. Where did Operation Overlord start? _______________

15. Who was the Supreme Allied Commander in 1944? _______________

16. When was D-day? _______________

17. Who was the "Desert Fox"? _______________ What forces did he command
    and where? _______________

18. What was a "cricket"? Who used it? When? _______________
    _______________

19. Where did the "bulge" occur in the Battle of the Bulge? _______________

20. Who massacred millions from racial and ethnic groups, and what was that massacre
    called? _______________

21. When was the bomb dropped on Hiroshima? _______________

22. When was the bomb dropped on Nagasaki? _______________

23. What was the turning point of the Japanese offensive? _______________

24. Who took over the presidency upon FDR's death? _______________

25. What was the name of the plane that dropped the first bomb? _______________

26. What was the German word for their armed forces? _______________

27. What was the German word for their air force? _______________

28. Where was the "great arsenal of democracy"? _______________

29. What is *Anschluss?* _______________

30. In Norway, whose name is synonymous with *traitor?* _______________

31. What committees did the pacifists and isolationists organize? _______________

32. When did the Yalta meeting of the Big Three take place? _______________

33. Who were the Big Three? _______________

34. What issue did the Russian leader at Yalta agree to but not practice? _______________
_______________

35. Who were *kamikazes?* _______________
_______________

36. When did Hitler write a book? _______________

37. What was it called? _______________

38. Who headed the U.S. Army, and who headed the U.S. Navy on the Pacific front?
_______________

39. What occurred on a national scale in 1943 to help improve the government's tax flow? _______________

40. Where did the "death march" occur in World War II? _______________
_______________

41. Who were the two new faces at Potsdam? _______________

42. What was the one item upon which they agreed? _______________
_______________

43. Where did Operation Torch take place? _______________

44. Who commanded that mission? _______________

45. When did the War Production Board begin? _______________

46. What was its function? _______________

47. What was the most significant Pacific conquest of summer 1944? _______________
_______________ What effect did it have on the future fight? _______________
_______________

48. What act set aside $7 billion to supply embattled nations? _______________

49. Who gave a speech about four freedoms? _______________ What were his "Four Freedoms"? _______________

## To Win or Not to Win

**General Douglas MacArthur and President Truman had a falling out after MacArthur made statements that were critical of the administration's decisions in the Korean War. After his dismissal, MacArthur spoke to a joint session of Congress and made the statement, "In war, indeed, there can be no substitute for victory." Evaluate that statement in light of the following questions.**

1. Read Luke 14:28-32. According to that passage, is MacArthur's statement correct? Explain. ________________________________________________________________

   ________________________________________________________________

   ________________________________________________________________

   ________________________________________________________________

   What principle is this passage teaching? ________________________________

   ________________________________________________________________

2. At the end of World War I and World War II, what do you think was the overall attitude of the civilians and veterans toward what had been accomplished? Do you think it was the same after the Korean and Vietnam Wars? If it was different, what made the difference? Does this support or weaken General MacArthur's statement? Explain.

   ________________________________________________________________

   ________________________________________________________________

   ________________________________________________________________

   ________________________________________________________________

   ________________________________________________________________

   ________________________________________________________________

   ________________________________________________________________

   ________________________________________________________________

   ________________________________________________________________

3. Did the Korean War effectively contain the threat of communism in Asia? Explain.

   ________________________________________________________________

   ________________________________________________________________

   ________________________________________________________________

   ________________________________________________________________

4. What possible differences would there have been in world affairs if the United States had won a decisive victory in Korea? Explain. ____________________________

   ________________________________________________________________

   ________________________________________________________________

   ________________________________________________________________

## Map Study: The Korean War

**Refer to a world atlas and/or an encyclopedia to complete the map.**

1. Locate and label the following:

   Countries—China, Manchuria, North Korea, South Korea
   Places—Seoul, Inchon, Yalu River, Panmunjom

2. Label the following:

   Boundaries—38th Parallel, 1953 Armistice Line, the line showing the farthest
   advance of U.N. forces into North Korea

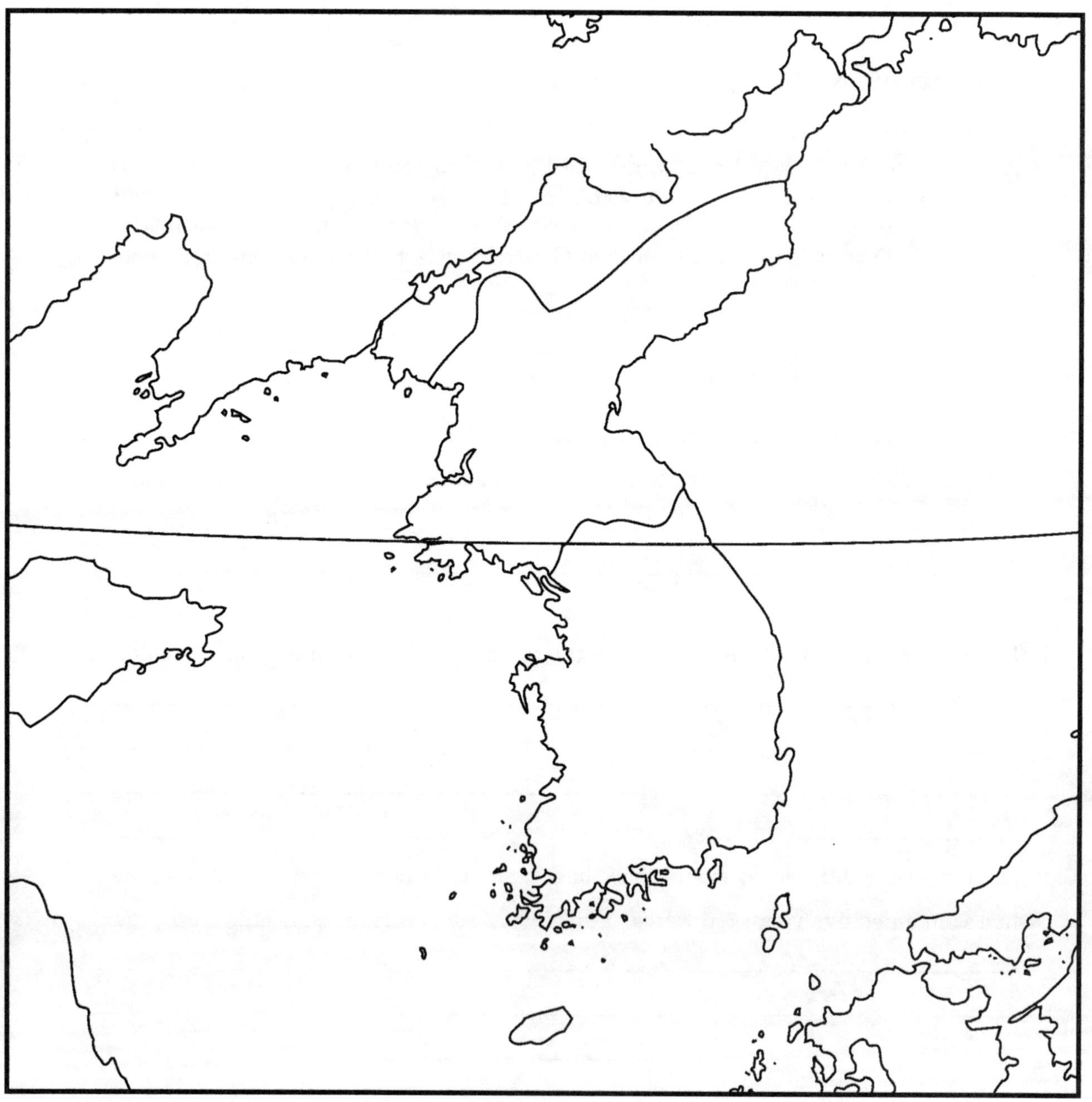

## Advertising Anomalies

**With televisions in many homes, the 1950s saw the onset of advertising on an unprecedented scale. Today, many consumers buy products based on the brand name, the packaging, the jingle, the endorsements, or how the product will enhance their image. Christians need to be good stewards of God's money and buy a product based on its worth. In the following exercise, analyze three different brands of the same food product. Answer the questions about each brand and draw your conclusion at the end. Answers will vary depending on the students' choices.**

What is the product's brand name? ______________________________

Do you know anything about this product from advertising? If so, what did the

advertising say about the product? _____________________________

_________________________________________________________

How does its packaging appeal to you? (color, type style, picture, shape) __________

_________________________________________________________

_________________________________________________________

What are this product's ingredients? ___________________________

_________________________________________________________

On a scale of 1 to 5, 5 being highest, how would you rate this product's taste? ________

What was the cost of this product per ounce? ____________________

What is the product's brand name? ______________________________

Do you know anything about this product from advertising? If so, what did the

advertising say about the product? _____________________________

_________________________________________________________

How does its packaging appeal to you? (color, type style, picture, shape) __________

_________________________________________________________

_________________________________________________________

What are this product's ingredients? ___________________________

_________________________________________________________

On a scale of 1 to 5, 5 being highest, how would you rate this product's taste? ________

What was the cost of this product per ounce? ____________________

What is the product's brand name? _______________________________________

Do you know anything about this product from advertising? If so, what did the

advertising say about the product? _______________________________________

_______________________________________________________________________

How does its packaging appeal to you? (color, type style, picture, shape)

_______________________________________________________________________

_______________________________________________________________________

What are this product's ingredients? ____________________________________

_______________________________________________________________________

On a scale of 1 to 5, 5 being highest, how would you rate this product's taste? _______

What was the cost of this product per ounce? ____________________________

## Analysis

Which product would you have bought prior to analysis? __________________

What would your motivation for purchase have been? ______________________

Which product is most expensive? ______________________________________

How do you think advertising affected the cost of this product? ____________

_______________________________________________________________________

Which product, if any, tastes best? _____________________________________

Which product, if any, is most visually appealing? _______________________

Based on calories, fat grams, and nutritional content, which product, if any, is most nutritious?

_______________________________________________________________________

Based on all the information you have gathered, which product is the best buy for your

money? (Defend your decision.) ________________________________________

_______________________________________________________________________

_______________________________________________________________________

_______________________________________________________________________

_______________________________________________________________________

_______________________________________________________________________

## Optional Discussion

What makes a brand of clothing popular? Is it more comfortable than comparable non-brand items? How do you determine if an item is popular? Why does popularity change the price of an item? What do brand names say about you if you wear them?

## "Red and Yellow, Black and White"

**In 1908, the British author Israel Zangwill produced a play in which one of the characters said, "America is God's great melting pot where all the races of Europe are melting and re-forming!" Since that time, immigrants have poured into America from every nation in the world, bringing an ethnic diversity that sometimes doesn't melt away. This diversity is often the cause of misunderstanding, conflict, and sometimes violence. In the 1960s, the conflict came to the attention of the American people in the form of the civil rights movement, but even now it continues to breed controversy. The Bible has much to say about how we react to others. Study the Scripture verses below and answer the questions on the next page.**

1. Write a two- or three-sentence summary of how God deals with diverse people and cultures in each of the following Scripture passages.

   • I Samuel 16:7

   • Matthew 7:15-20

   • Romans 10:1-13

   • I Corinthians 3:10-15

   • 1 Corinthians 12:1-27

   • James 2:1-9

2. Based on these passages, do you think culture or race affects a person's ability to be saved? Support your answer with Scripture. _______________________________________

_______________________________________

_______________________________________

3. Once you are saved, how does God judge you? Support your answer with Scripture.

_______________________________________

_______________________________________

4. Look up the word *prejudice* in a dictionary and write a general definition. _____________

_______________________________________

_______________________________________

5. Write at least five groups that people are prejudiced against. Include more than just racial groups. _______________________________________

_______________________________________

_______________________________________

_______________________________________

_______________________________________

6. Do you think that a prejudice about a group of people affects a person's willingness to witness or minister to that group? Explain why or why not. Which most affects your witness? _______________________________________

_______________________________________

_______________________________________

_______________________________________

_______________________________________

_______________________________________

_______________________________________

### Optional Activity

**Topic #1**
Should a person who has tested HIV positive be allowed to enroll in your school?

**Topic #2**
You come late to camp, and you need a room. You see that there are two rooms with only one person in them. In one room is the richest kid in the youth group; in the other room is this kid who rides the bus from the worst part of town to come to church every Sunday. You do not know either kid well. With whom should you room?

**Topic #3**
A couple has been waiting to adopt a baby for eight years. The adoption agency calls and says they have a baby for them. When they arrive, they find that the baby has a severely deformed leg but, other than that, is beautiful. Should they adopt the child?



126

## Postwar Events

**Put the letter for the correct date next to the event.**

_______ 1. Truman becomes president of the United States

_______ 2. South Korea is invaded by North Korea

_______ 3. Fidel Castro overthrows the Cuban dictator

_______ 4. construction of Berlin Wall begins

_______ 5. John F. Kennedy takes the oath of office

_______ 6. civil rights march on Washington, D.C.

_______ 7. McCarthyism

_______ 8. Cuban Missile Crisis

_______ 9. Bay of Pigs

_______ 10. Iron Curtain descends on Eastern Europe

_______ 11. Berlin Airlift forces the end of the Soviet blockade

_______ 12. H-bomb developed

_______ 13. truce between North and South Korea begins

_______ 14. "one nation under God" is added to Pledge of Allegiance

_______ 15. United Nations begins

_______ 16. Dwight D. Eisenhower takes the presidential oath

_______ 17. NATO is formed

_______ 18. Warsaw Pact is established

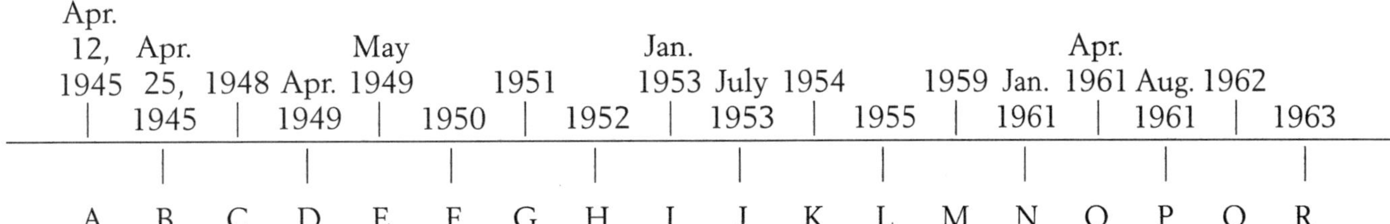

## Who Am I?

**Read each statement and decide who would have said it. Write his or her name in the blank.**

________________________ 1. I was the gifted black athlete who accepted the challenge to integrate professional baseball.

________________________ 2. I was a former State Department official who was accused of passing secret documents to a Soviet spy.

________________________ 3. Under my leadership, the Communist Chinese gained control of mainland China.

________________________ 4. The *Chicago Daily Tribune* printed what everyone expected when it mistakenly headlined that I had defeated Truman.

________________________ 5. I started the Peace Corps as part of my New Frontier legislative program.

________________________ 6. I created a Communist state just ninety miles from the Florida coast.

________________________ 7. I gained worldwide fame after a tent meeting in Los Angeles.

________________________ 8. In Little Rock, Arkansas, I used the National Guard to block nine black students from going to the local high school.

________________________ 9. I founded the *National Review*, a magazine that promotes conservative views.

________________________ 10. The Berlin Wall was constructed under my leadership.

________________________ 11. I led the Nationalist Chinese and headed that government in exile in Taiwan.

________________________ 12. I expanded the New Deal and called my legislative program the Fair Deal.

________________________ 13. I headed a Senate subcommittee to investigate whether or not Communists were present in our government.

________________________ 14. We helped give classified information about the atomic bomb to the Soviets.

________________________ 15. With my vice president, Richard Nixon, I won the 1952 election by a landslide.

________________________ 16. Influenced by Mahatma Gandhi and Henry David Thoreau, I supported using nonviolent resistance and civil disobedience in the civil rights movement.

________________________ 17. My child-care book popularized the theories of Freud and Dewey and was outsold only by the Bible.

________________________ 18. I refused to give my bus seat to a white man. My arrest led to a bus boycott in Montgomery, Alabama.

________________________ 19. After the president fired me, I ran against him on the Progressive ticket in the 1948 election.

## The Johnson Years—Salving Society's Ills

**Answer the following questions about pages 564-67 of the text.**

1. What was the goal of Johnson's "Great Society"? _______________________

    _______________________________________________________________

2. What was the first and most important of Johnson's civil rights bills? _______

    _______________________________________________________________

    A. List four racial injustices it hoped to end. _______________________

    _______________________________________________________________

    _______________________________________________________________

    B. What did the bill create to ensure nondiscrimination in hiring practices? _______

    _______________________________________________________________

3. In the next year, what act would help give black Americans more political power? ____

    _______________________________________________________________

4. What department did Johnson use to attack poverty? _______________________

    _______________________________________________________________

5. In what three ways did the government attack poverty? _______________________

    _______________________________________________________________

6. What allowed Johnson to push eighty-nine bills through the legislature in 1965? ______

    _______________________________________________________________

7. Which one of those bills would have the widest impact on the nation? _______________

8. What was the policy of the Supreme Court in the 1960s called? _______________

9. Name the five civil rights cases for which the Warren Court is best known. After the
   case name, write in your own words what happened as a result of each case.

    A. _______________________________________________________________

    _______________________________________________________________

    B. _______________________________________________________________

    _______________________________________________________________

    C. _______________________________________________________________

    _______________________________________________________________

    D. _______________________________________________________________

    _______________________________________________________________

    E. _______________________________________________________________

    _______________________________________________________________

## Map Study: War in Vietnam

**Refer to the map on page 569 of the text to complete this activity.**

1.  Label the following locations.

    Countries—North Vietnam, South Vietnam, China, Burma, Laos, Thailand, Cambodia

    Places—Gulf of Tonkin, Gulf of Siam, Hanoi, Haiphong, Saigon, Mekong Delta, Phnom Penh

2.  Draw the Ho Chi Minh Trail and the DMZ on the map.

3.  Answer the following questions.

    Why was it called the Tet Offensive? _________________________________________

    What was napalm? __________________________________________________________

    Who were the Viet Cong? ____________________________________________________

    What occurred as a result of the incident in the Gulf of Tonkin? ____________________

    ___________________________________________________________________________

    ___________________________________________________________________________

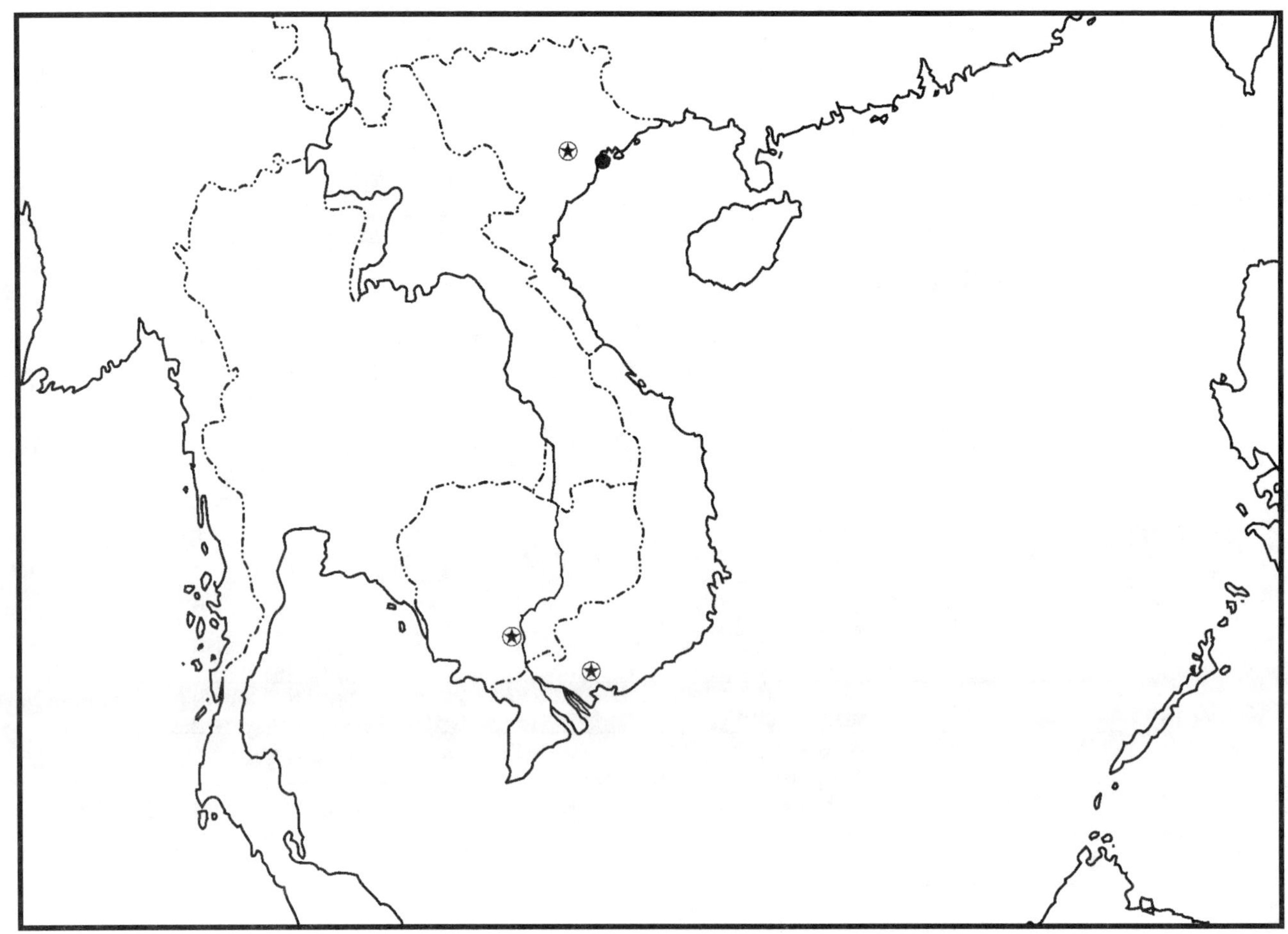

# UNITED STATES HISTORY

## The Bible as a Guidebook

**We know that man is inherently sinful and, therefore, incapable of producing a perfect society. Yet we also know that God says He will bless those who keep His ways (Prov. 8:32). In this exercise you are to give scriptural ways of dealing with social problems. Phrase your answers as if you were speaking to the group listed.**

1. The problem of hiring discrimination or pay discrimination against minorities

   • To the person discriminating _______________________________________

   _______________________________________________________________________

   _______________________________________________________________________

   _______________________________________________________________________

   _______________________________________________________________________

   • To the person being discriminated against ___________________________

   _______________________________________________________________________

   _______________________________________________________________________

   _______________________________________________________________________

   _______________________________________________________________________

2. The problem of poverty

   • To the financially comfortable _____________________________________

   _______________________________________________________________________

   _______________________________________________________________________

   _______________________________________________________________________

   _______________________________________________________________________

   • To the poor _________________________________________________________

   _______________________________________________________________________

   _______________________________________________________________________

   _______________________________________________________________________

   _______________________________________________________________________

3.  The care of the elderly

• To the young _______________________________________________

_______________________________________________

_______________________________________________

_______________________________________________

_______________________________________________

• To the elderly _______________________________________________

_______________________________________________

_______________________________________________

_______________________________________________

_______________________________________________

4.  The problem of civil disobedience

• To those using it for change _______________________________________________

_______________________________________________

_______________________________________________

_______________________________________________

_______________________________________________

• To the Christian _______________________________________________

_______________________________________________

_______________________________________________

_______________________________________________

_______________________________________________

## Space Race Matching

**Match each of the phrases with the person, thing, or event it describes. Some letters will not be used, and some will be used more than once.**

_______ 1. He spent thirty-four hours in orbit.

_______ 2. Germany's rocket pioneer

_______ 3. code name for project designed to lift man into orbit

_______ 4. had two hatches to allow for space walks

_______ 5. president who initially committed U.S. resources to the space program

_______ 6. lunar module name

_______ 7. Goddard's nickname

_______ 8. world's first satellite

_______ 9. fuel for Goddard's early rockets

_______ 10. von Braun bomb development used to blitz London

_______ 11. project designed to put two men into orbit

_______ 12. His flight landed less than four miles off target.

_______ 13. the first man on the moon

_______ 14 number of feet the first rocket flew

_______ 15. He helped finance Goddard's experiments.

_______ 16. father of American rocketry

_______ 17. first American to orbit in space

_______ 18. *Eagle* was part of this space project.

_______ 19. first American to walk in space

_______ 20. command module name

A. Apollo
B. *Columbia*
C. *Eagle*
D. Edward White
E. Gemini
F. Gordon Cooper
G. gunpowder and alcohol
H. John Glenn Jr.
I. Kennedy
J. Lindbergh
K. Mercury
L. "Moony"
M. Neil Armstrong
N. Nixon
O. oxygen and gasoline
P. Robert H. Goddard
Q. "Spacey"
R. *Sputnik 1*
S. V-2
T. Walter Schirra
U. Werner von Braun
V. 184 feet
W. 236 feet
X. 1926
Y. 1935

## What Ever Happened to . . . ?

**Using an encyclopedia or the Internet, locate information on America's seven original astronauts. Find out briefly where their space careers led them.**

1. Walter M. Schirra, Jr.—

2. Donald K. Slayton—

3. John H. Glenn, Jr.—

4. Scott Carpenter—

5. Alan B. Shepard, Jr.—

6. Virgil I. "Gus" Grissom—

7. L. Gordon Cooper—

## A Woman's Place

There is much controversy over the place of women in society today. On one hand, there are those who say that a woman should be able to pursue anything she chooses with no extra burdens of home responsibilities. On the other hand, there are those who say that a woman should never work outside the home. The Scriptures should be the ultimate guide for making decisions; therefore, it is imperative to know the principles found in God's Word. Answer the questions below and then use the Bible and a concordance to write your philosophy concerning a woman's place in society. It may be useful to discuss the Christian woman's role in society with your parents, pastor, youth pastor, Bible teacher, or other respected Christians.

1. List at least three reasons women give for not working outside the home. ____________

    ________________________________________________

    ________________________________________________

2. List at least three complications in a woman's life that can result from not working outside the home. ____________

    ________________________________________________

    ________________________________________________

3. List three benefits which can come to a woman's life and family from her not working outside the home. ____________

    ________________________________________________

    ________________________________________________

4. What are three jobs that women can do in their homes to help financially? ____________

    ________________________________________________

5. How can a husband and/or children be supportive of a woman's decision not to work outside the home? ____________

    ________________________________________________

    ________________________________________________

6. On a separate sheet of paper, make a chart comparing the advantages and disadvantages of working in the home, especially dealing with time, money, and emotional, social, physical, and spiritual considerations.

7. List at least five improvements in technology in the past fifty years that have reduced a woman's workload at home. ____________

    ________________________________________________

    ________________________________________________

8. List at least three reasons women give for working outside the home.______

______

______

9. List three complications in a woman's life that can result from working outside the home. ______

______

______

10. List three benefits that working outside the home can bring to a woman's life and family. ______

______

______

11. How can a husband and/or children help a woman balance home chores and outside work? ______

______

______

12. On a separate sheet of paper, make a chart comparing the advantages and disadvantages of working outside the home, especially dealing with time, money, and emotional, social, physical, and spiritual considerations.

13. According to the Scriptures, what are some of a woman's responsibilities in marriage?

______

______

______

14. Does a woman's role change as her life progresses? Explain. (Consider marriage, birth of children, death of or divorce from a spouse, and marriage of children.) ______

______

______

______

______

______

15. In Proverbs 31:10-31, find at least five character traits that mark God's example of a virtuous woman. ______

______

______

16. On a separate sheet of paper, write your philosophy (belief) of what a woman's place in society should be. Support it with Scripture. Titus 2:3-5 and I Peter 3:1-12 are good places to begin.

## Three Men and the Presidency

**Place the following information into the chart below the president it describes.**

unelected president
peanut farmer
pardoned former president
oil embargo
defense of human rights
House minority leader
John C. Calhoun
"born-again" claim
outsider to Washington
Iranian hostages

Panama Canal Treaty
final defeat in Vietnam
Camp David Accords
Ayatollah Khomeini
ended gold standard
SALT II Treaty
resignation
high unemployment rate
sweaters and jeans
hostile Congress

golfing accident
George McGovern
football player
granted amnesty
Watergate affair
veto
Spiro Agnew
Daniel Ellsberg
12%-13% inflation

| NIXON | FORD | CARTER |
|---|---|---|
|  |  |  |
|  |  |  |
|  |  |  |
|  |  |  |
|  |  |  |
|  |  |  |
|  |  |  |
|  |  |  |
|  |  |  |
|  |  |  |

## The Christian and Politics

**The New Right included a large portion of conservative Christians who began to voice their views in the political arena. Answer the following questions about the effect of Christianity on government.**

1. Refer to pages 82, 235, 482, 611-13, and 643-44 of the text. Next to each religious movement, list its social or political effect.

   a. First Great Awakening          a. _______________________________

   _______________________________________________

   _______________________________________________

   b. Second Great Awakening       b. _______________________________

   _______________________________________________

   _______________________________________________

   c. Fundamentalist Rise             c. _______________________________

   _______________________________________________

   _______________________________________________

   d. Religious Right                    d. _______________________________

   _______________________________________________

   _______________________________________________

2. Why do you think that political reform is often the result of religious reform? _______

   _______________________________________________

   _______________________________________________

3. Can we ever expect the world's political system to reach perfection? Why or why not?

   _______________________________________________

   _______________________________________________

   _______________________________________________

4. Should the Christian be involved in politics? ____________ Explain your answer with

   Scripture. _______________________________________

   _______________________________________________

   _______________________________________________

5. What can you do to make an impact on politics now? ____________________

   _______________________________________________

   _______________________________________________

## A Decade of Political Disaster

**The 1970s were filled with domestic and foreign disaster for the American people. Answer the following questions.**

1. What other presidents that you have studied were plagued by scandals in their administrations? ________________________________________

2. What character trait did Ford have that Nixon hoped would help his administration?
   ________________________________________

3. What single event devastated Ford's early popularity? ________________________________________

4. Why was Congress so determined to maintain control during Ford's administration?
   ________________________________________

5. What does OPEC stand for? ________________________________________

6. Why did OPEC call for an oil embargo? ________________________________________
   ________________________________________

7. What caused gasoline to be scarce during the early days of the embargo? ________________________________________
   ________________________________________

8. Why did the prices skyrocket later? ________________________________________
   ________________________________________

9. How did environmental concerns contribute to the energy crisis? ________________________________________
   ________________________________________

10. Define *stagflation*. ________________________________________
    ________________________________________

11. What were three causes of stagflation? ________________________________________
    ________________________________________

12. What occurred in 1971 that seemed to make it necessary for Nixon to end the gold standard? ________________________________________

13. When the gold standard was dropped, what happened to the value of the dollar?
    ________________________________________

14. What three things contributed to Gerald Ford's loss in the 1976 election? ________________________________________
    ________________________________________

15. What decision caused Carter to lose the approval of veterans? ________________________________________
    ________________________________________

16. What was central to Carter's foreign policy? _______________________________

_______________________________________________________________________

17. What were the terms of the Panama Canal Treaty? ___________________________

_______________________________________________________________________

_______________________________________________________________________

18. What was the peace agreement between Israel and Egypt called? ______________

19. What did Egypt agree to in those talks? ___________________________________

_______________________________________________________________________

20. What did Israel agree to? ______________________________________________

_______________________________________________________________________

21. Was the SALT II Treaty ever ratified? ____________________________________

22. What action by the Soviets greatly affected the SALT II decision? _____________

_______________________________________________________________________

23. What was the "Carter Doctrine"? ________________________________________

_______________________________________________________________________

24. Who was the Islamic extremist who denounced the United States as "the great Satan"?

_______________________________________________________________________

25. Why did Iran take American hostages? ____________________________________

_______________________________________________________________________

26. How many hostages were taken? _________________________________________

27. How many days did the Americans remain hostage? _________________________

28. Who campaigned against Carter for the Democratic nomination in the election of
1980? __________________________________________________________________

29. What liberal Republican ran as an independent third-party candidate? ___________

30. Who won the presidential election of 1980? ________________________________

## Map Study: The Reagan Doctrine in Central America and the Caribbean

**Refer to the map on page 625 of the text to complete the map below.**

1. Label the following countries:

   | Costa Rica | El Salvador | Guatemala | Nicaragua |
   |---|---|---|---|
   | Cuba | Grenada | Panama | |

2. Use green to color the country that the United States helped with arms and advice and economic aid.

3. Use red to color the country that supplied arms to the Salvadoran rebels.

4. Use yellow to color the Caribbean country that, with the support of the Soviets, backed the Sandinista guerrillas.

5. If the Central American countries had fallen to communism, what strategic shipping lane may also have gone into Communist hands? ______________________________

   Use blue to color it.

## The First Four Years

**Put the letter of the correct answer in the blank. Then answer the questions at the bottom of the page. Answers may be used once or more than once.**

_______ 1. Mujahideen

_______ 2. tough stance against Communist aggression

_______ 3. lower unemployment, interest, and oil prices

_______ 4. Leon Klinghoffer killed

_______ 5. automatic deficit reduction plan

_______ 6. Maurice Bishop

_______ 7. income tax cut 25% over $2\frac{1}{2}$ year period

_______ 8. cut taxes and reduced government regulation

_______ 9. Sandinistas vs. the Contras

_______ 10. amount of proposed budget cuts

_______ 11. PLO involvement

_______ 12. Jonas Savimbi

_______ 13. supply-side economics

_______ 14. toy truck bombs

_______ 15. amount of interest payments on debts

A. *Achille Lauro*

B. Afghanistan

C. Angola

D. Economic Recovery Tax Act

E. El Salvador

F. Gramm-Rudman Act

G. Grenada

H. Lebanon

I. limited-government agenda

J. Reagonomics

K. Reagan Doctrine

L. Roaring 80s

M. $35 billion

N. $150 billion

16. What problem caused the Gramm-Rudman Act to be less effective than it might have been? _______________________________________________

_______________________________________________

17. What was the chemical weapon used in Afghanistan called? _______________

18. What event caused the United States peace-keeping forces to withdraw from Lebanon? _______________________________________________

_______________________________________________

19. Explain supply-side economics in your own words. _______________________

_______________________________________________

_______________________________________________

_______________________________________________

20. What were the two points of the Reagan Revolution? _______________________

_______________________________________________

21. In spite of all the budget cut demands, what area received a boost in spending, and how much money did it receive? _______________________________________________

## This or That

**Underline the choice that will make the statement correct.**

1. Hungary / Poland was the first Communist-bloc country to open the way for free elections.

2. Geraldine Ferraro was the first woman vice-presidential candidate / appointed to the Supreme Court.

3. *Glasnost / Perestroika* gave the Russians a thirst for freedom and renewed nationalism.

4. INF / SDI / START was a proposed space-based defense system.

5. The "Reagan Revolution" / Reaganomics had two points stating that America must be strong and free.

6. The INF treaty / START agreement eliminated most medium-range missiles from Europe.

7. President Reagan began funneling supplies to Angola / Grenada to aid in stopping Cuban and Soviet influence.

8. When it opened its western borders, Hungary / Poland became an escape route for East Germans and Rumanians.

9. The meetings between the Soviet Union and the United States to cut the size of long-range nuclear arsenals were called INF / START / SDI.

10. The Mujahideen were guerrilla forces the Soviets tried to stop in Iraq / Afghanistan.

11. Reagan's second-term election was a 49 to 1 / 28 to 22 state victory.

12. Qaddafi / Khomeini, leader of Libya, was surprised when the United States responded to his support of terrorism with air strikes.

13. The undercover use of money from the sale of arms to aid in the battle against the Communist Sandinistas became the object of an investigation into Just Cause / the Iran-Contra affair.

14. The focus of Reagan's second term was on foreign / domestic affairs.

15. John Poindexter's / Oliver North's indictment in the Iran-Contra affair was overturned in 1990.

16. On November 9, 1989, the Iron Curtain / Berlin Wall ceased to be a barrier and opened the way for German reunification.

17. *Glasnost / Perestroika* was the restructuring of the Communist economy.

18. The election of George Bush to the presidency was in many ways a last show of approval for Ronald Reagan / Dan Quayle.

19. The governor of Massachusetts, Jack Kemp / Michael Dukakis, ran against Bush in the 1988 election.

20. The Soviet head of state who brought *glasnost* to the Soviet society was Leonid Brezhnev / Mikhail Gorbachev.

## Map Study: Operation Desert Storm

**Refer to the map on page 635 of the text to complete the map below.**

1. Label the following countries:

   | | | | | |
   |---|---|---|---|---|
   | Egypt | Iran | Jordan | Lebanon | Syria |
   | Iraq | Israel | Kuwait | Saudi Arabia | |

2. Label the following cities:

   | | | |
   |---|---|---|
   | Baghdad | Jerusalem | Tel Aviv |
   | Cairo | Kuwait City | |

3. Use red to color the country that Iraq invaded.

4. Why was this country worth going to war over? ______________________

   ________________________________________________________________

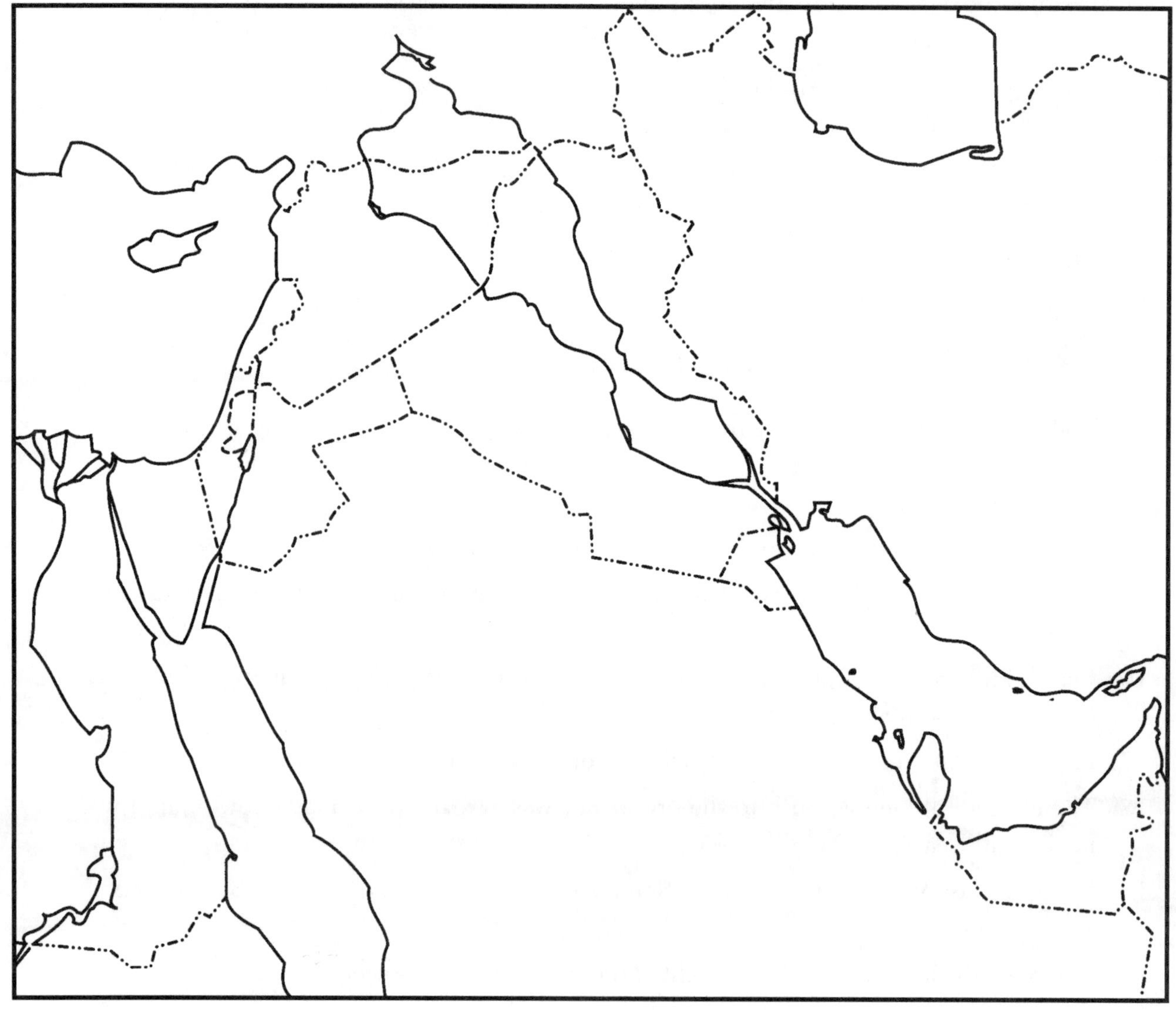

## The Gulf War Presidential Address

**On Wednesday, January 16, 1991, President Bush addressed the nation concerning the bombing of Iraq. In his speech the president included the reasons for U.S. involvement and goals to be achieved. Read the excerpt from his speech and list his reasons and goals.**

Five months ago, Saddam Hussein started this cruel war against Kuwait; tonight the battle has been joined. This military action, taken in accord with United Nations resolutions and with the consent of the United States Congress, follows months of constant and virtually endless diplomatic activity on the part of the United Nations, the United States and many, many other countries.

Arab leaders sought what became known as an Arab solution, only to conclude that Saddam Hussein was unwilling to leave Kuwait. Others traveled to Baghdad in a variety of efforts to restore peace and justice. Our Secretary of State, James Baker, held an historic meeting in Geneva only to be totally rebuffed.

Now, the 28 countries with forces in the gulf area have exhausted all reasonable efforts to reach a peaceful resolution, have no choice but to drive Saddam from Kuwait by force. We will not fail.

As I report to you, air attacks are under way against military targets in Iraq. We are determined to knock out Saddam Hussein's nuclear bomb potential. We will also destroy his chemical weapons facilities. Much of Saddam's artillery and tanks will be destroyed.

Our objectives are clear. Saddam Hussein's forces will leave Kuwait. The legitimate government of Kuwait will be restored to its rightful place, and Kuwait will once again be free.

Sanctions, though having some effect, showed no signs of accomplishing their objectives. Sanctions were tried for well over five months, and we and our allies concluded that sanctions alone would not force Saddam from Kuwait.

While the world waited, Saddam Hussein systematically raped, pillaged, and plundered a tiny nation—no threat to his own. He subjected the people of Kuwait to unspeakable atrocities, and among those maimed and murdered—innocent children. While the world waited, Saddam sought to add to the chemical weapons arsenal [that] he now possesses an infinitely more dangerous weapon of mass destruction, a nuclear weapon.

And while the world waited, while the world talked peace and withdrawal, Saddam Hussein dug in and moved massive forces into Kuwait. While the world waited, while Saddam stalled, more damage was being done to the fragile economies of the Third World, the emerging democracies of Eastern Europe, to the entire world, including to our own economy.

The United States, together with the United Nations, exhausted every means at our disposal to bring this crisis to a peaceful end.

I'm hopeful that this fighting will not go on for long and that casualties will be held to an absolute minimum. This is an historic moment. We have in this past year made great progress in ending the long era of conflict and Cold War. We have before us the opportunity to forge for ourselves and for future generations a new world order, a world where the rule of law, not the law of the jungle, governs the conduct of nations. When we are successful, and we will be, we have a real chance at this new world order, an order in which a credible United Nations can use its peacekeeping role to fulfill the promise and vision of the UN's founders.

It is my hope that somehow the Iraqi people can even now convince their dictator that he must lay down his arms, leave Kuwait, and let Iraq itself rejoin the family of peace-loving nations.

And let me say to everyone listening or watching tonight: When the troops we've sent in finish their work, I'm determined to bring them home as soon as possible. Tonight, as our forces fight, they and their families are in our prayers.

May God bless each and every one of them and the coalition forces at our side in the Gulf, and may He continue to bless our nation, the United States of America.

1. Reasons for: _______________________________________________

\
\
\
\
\
\
\
\
\
\
\
\
\
\
\
\
\
\
\

2. Goals: _______________________________________________

\
\
\
\
\
\
\
\
\
\
\
\
\
\
\
\
\
\
\

## Opposition and Support

**As President Clinton began his first term in office, he initiated several policies. Chart the description of each policy and identify whether it was supported or opposed by Congress.**

| Policy | Description | Supported/Opposed |
|---|---|---|
| "Don't Ask, Don't Tell" | | |
| Family and Medical Leave Act | | |
| Brady Bill | | |
| National Voter Registration Act | | |
| NAFTA | | |
| Health Care | | |

## Questions and Answers

**Answer the following questions using the textbook and reference materials.**

1. Why was President Clinton referred to as "the comeback kid"?

   ___________________________________________________________

   ___________________________________________________________

   ___________________________________________________________

   ___________________________________________________________

2. Why did one Democratic congressman say that if a person did not like President Clinton's position on a particular issue, he needed only to wait a few weeks?

   ___________________________________________________________

   ___________________________________________________________

   ___________________________________________________________

3. How did signing the Defense of Marriage Act hurt Clinton's endorsement of homosexual rights?

   ___________________________________________________________

   ___________________________________________________________

   ___________________________________________________________

4. When and how did President Clinton present himself as a New Democrat?

   ___________________________________________________________

   ___________________________________________________________

   ___________________________________________________________

5. Why did the Supreme Court strike down the line-item veto?

   ___________________________________________________________

   ___________________________________________________________

   ___________________________________________________________

6. What negative character qualities do some of the previous questions' answers illustrate about President Clinton?

   ___________________________________________________________

   ___________________________________________________________

   ___________________________________________________________

## Dayton Accords

**The following fundamental rights and freedoms are from the Dayton Peace Accords on Bosnia. Using the Declaration of Independence, the Bill of Rights, and Amendment 13 identify specific phrases that correspond to the Dayton Accords Rights and Freedoms.**

### *Dayton Accords Rights and Freedoms*

1. Right to life.—_______________________________________________

_______________________________________________________________

2. Right not to be subjected to torture or inhuman or degrading treatment or

   punishment.—__________________________________________________

_______________________________________________________________

3. Right not to be held in slavery or servitude or to perform forced or compulsory

   labor.—_______________________________________________________

_______________________________________________________________

4. Rights to liberty and security of person.—______________________________

_______________________________________________________________

5. Right to a fair hearing in civil and criminal matters and other rights.—__________

_______________________________________________________________

6. Right to private and family life, home, and correspondence—________________

_______________________________________________________________

7. Freedom of thought, conscience, and religion.—__________________________

_______________________________________________________________

8. Freedom of expression.—___________________________________________

_______________________________________________________________

9. Freedom of peaceful assembly and freedom of association with others.—________

_______________________________________________________________

10. Right to marry and to found a family.—________________________________

_______________________________________________________________

11. Right to property.—______________________________________________

_______________________________________________________________

12. Right to education.—_____________________________________________

_______________________________________________________________

13. Right to liberty of movement and residence.—___________________________

_______________________________________________________________

14. No discrimination on any grounds to prevent the enjoyment of the rights and freedoms.—_______________________________________________

_______________________________________________

## Discussion

1. List those freedoms or rights not specifically stated in the Declaration or Constitution:

_______________________________________________

_______________________________________________

_______________________________________________

2. For class discussion:

    a) Why were the Dayton Accords so specific with regard to the rights and freedoms listed in the previous question?

    _______________________________________________

    _______________________________________________

    _______________________________________________

    _______________________________________________

    _______________________________________________

    _______________________________________________

    b) Why were some freedoms and rights not specifically stated in the U.S. Constitution?

    _______________________________________________

    _______________________________________________

    c) Which groups of people in the United States were not privileged to these specific rights prior to 1865?

    _______________________________________________

    _______________________________________________

    d) Which freedom did the Proclamation Line of 1763 hinder? (See p. 97 of the text.)

    _______________________________________________

    _______________________________________________

## Clinton Foreign Policy

**Identify the countries in which President Clinton placed U.S. troops or maintained their presence in conjunction with his foreign policy. Chart the country, military involvement and reasons for being there, and the result.**

| Country | Military Involvement and Reasons | Result |
|---------|----------------------------------|--------|
|         |                                  |        |
|         |                                  |        |
|         |                                  |        |
|         |                                  |        |

## What Do You Remember?

**Identify each of the following.**

______________________ 1. Secured federal benefits for spouses in traditional marriages only

______________________ 2. Ten popular bills House Republicans promised to bring up for a vote

______________________ 3. Conservative religious organization

______________________ 4. Would allow the president to eliminate specific spending items in the federal budget

______________________ 5. Rising political force seeking ways to secure legal recognition of the homosexual lifestyle

______________________ 6. Network of local servers connected electronically around the world

______________________ 7. Event dominating the second term of President Clinton

______________________ 8. In charge of a task force to plan the best way to implement health care reform

______________________ 9. Most significant scandal of the Clinton presidency; led to great humiliation in second term

______________________ 10. Required welfare recipients to go back to work within two years; placed a lifetime cap of five years for assistance

______________________ 11. 1996 Republican presidential candidate

______________________ 12. International network joining thousands of smaller networks into one

______________________ 13. Agreement fashioning Bosnia into a confederation in which Serbs, Croats, and Muslims shared power

______________________ 14. New force in America by which conservative views on political issues were expressed

______________________ 15. Yugoslavian province that became the scene of ethnic clashes

______________________ 16. Nickname of Bill Clinton reflecting his continued rebounding despite problems and scandals

______________________ 17. Legislation opening free trade with Mexico

______________________ 18. Country whose warlords baffled President Clinton, leading to a withdrawal of U.S. troops

______________________ 19. Reduced normal correspondence and telephone calls

______________________ 20. Presided over the impeachment trial of President Clinton

______________________ 21. One of Congress's most significant pieces of gun control legislation

______________________ 22. Conservative broadcast combining radio and religion

## 2001 Inaugural Address

**After reading excerpts from President George W. Bush's inaugural address, explain what you think the president meant.**

### *Excerpt 1:*

We have a place, all of us, in a long story—a story we continue, but whose end we will not see. It is the story of a new world that became a friend and liberator of the old, a story of a slave-holding society that became a servant of freedom, the story of a power that went into the world to protect but not possess, to defend but not to conquer.

_______________________________________________

_______________________________________________

_______________________________________________

_______________________________________________

_______________________________________________

### *Excerpt 2:*

Through much of the last century, America's faith in freedom and democracy was a rock in a raging sea. Now it is a seed upon the wind, taking root in many nations.

_______________________________________________

_______________________________________________

_______________________________________________

_______________________________________________

### *Excerpt 3:*

America has never been united by blood or birth or soil. We are bound by ideals that move us beyond our backgrounds, lift us above our interests and teach us what it means to be citizens. Every child must be taught these principles. Every citizen must uphold them. And every immigrant, by embracing these ideals, makes our country more, not less, American.

_______________________________________________

_______________________________________________

_______________________________________________

_______________________________________________

_______________________________________________

*Excerpt 4:*

Our national courage has been clear in times of depression and war, when defending common dangers defined our common good. Now we must choose if the example of our fathers and mothers will inspire us or condemn us. We must show courage in a time of blessing by confronting problems instead of passing them on to future generations.

_______________________________________________________________

_______________________________________________________________

_______________________________________________________________

_______________________________________________________________

_______________________________________________________________

*Excerpt 5:*

The enemies of liberty and our country should make no mistake: America remains engaged in the world by history and by choice, shaping a balance of power that favors freedom. We will defend our allies and our interests. We will show purpose without arrogance. We will meet aggression and bad faith with resolve and strength. And to all nations, we will speak for the values that gave our nation birth.

_______________________________________________________________

_______________________________________________________________

_______________________________________________________________

_______________________________________________________________

_______________________________________________________________

*Excerpt 6:*

And whatever our views of its cause, we can agree that children at risk are not at fault. Abandonment and abuse are not acts of God, they are failures of love.

_______________________________________________________________

_______________________________________________________________

_______________________________________________________________

_______________________________________________________________

_______________________________________________________________

*Excerpt 7:*

Government has great responsibilities for public safety and public health, for civil rights and common schools. Yet compassion is the work of a nation, not just a government.

_______________________________________________________________

_______________________________________________________________

_______________________________________________________________

_______________________________________________________________

_______________________________________________________________

### Excerpt 8:

And I pledge our nation to a goal: When we see that wounded traveler on the road to Jericho, we will not pass to the other side.

---

### Excerpt 9:

Our public interest depends on private character, on civic duty and family bonds and basic fairness, on uncounted, unhonored acts of decency which give direction to our freedom.

---

### Excerpt 10:

I will live and lead by these principles: to advance my convictions with civility, to pursue the public interest with courage, to speak for greater justice and compassion, to call for responsibility and try to live it as well.

---

### Excerpt 11:

What you do is as important as anything government does. I ask you to seek a common good beyond your comfort; to defend needed reforms against easy attacks; to serve your nation, beginning with your neighbor. I ask you to be citizens: citizens, not spectators; citizens, not subjects; responsible citizens, building communities of service and a nation of character.

*Excerpt 12:*

After the Declaration of Independence was signed, Virginia statesman John Page wrote to Thomas Jefferson: "We know the race is not to the swift nor the battle to the strong. Do you not think an angel rides in the whirlwind and directs this storm?"

________________________________________

________________________________________

________________________________________

________________________________________

________________________________________

*Excerpt 13:*

We are not this story's author, who fills time and eternity with his purpose. Yet his purpose is achieved in our duty, and our duty is fulfilled in service to one another.

________________________________________

________________________________________

________________________________________

________________________________________

________________________________________

*Excerpt 14:*

Never tiring, never yielding, never finishing, we renew that purpose today, to make our country more just and generous, to affirm the dignity of our lives and every life.

________________________________________

________________________________________

________________________________________

________________________________________

________________________________________

*Excerpt 15:*

This work continues. This story goes on. And an angel still rides in the whirlwind and directs the storm. God bless you all, and God bless America.

________________________________________

________________________________________

________________________________________

________________________________________

________________________________________